PRAYERS THAT BREAKTHROUGH:

UNLEASHING THE POWER OF PRAYER THROUGH

EFFECTIVELY PRAYING THE WORD

LENELAH MADDOX

WESTBOW®
PRESS
A DIVISION OF THOMAS NELSON
& ZONDERVAN

Scripture taken from the New King James Version. Copyright 1979, 1980, 1982 by Thomas Nelson, inc. Used by permission. All rights reserved.

Scripture taken from the King James Version of the Bible.

Scriptures taken from the Holy Bible, New International Version®, NIV®. Copyright © 1973, 1978, 1984, 2011 by Biblica, Inc.™ Used by permission of Zondervan. All rights reserved worldwide. www.zondervan.com The "NIV" and "New International Version" are trademarks registered in the United States Patent and Trademark Office by Biblica, Inc.™ All rights reserved.

Scripture quotations taken from the Holy Bible, New Living Translation, copyright 1996, 2004. Used by permission of Tyndale House Publishers, Inc., Wheaton, Illinois 60189. All rights reserved.

Scripture taken from The Living Bible copyright © 1971 by Tyndale House Foundation. Used by permission of Tyndale House Publishers Inc., Carol Stream, Illinois 60188. All rights reserved. The Living Bible, TLB, and the The Living Bible logo are registered trademarks of Tyndale House Publishers.

WestBow Press books may be ordered through booksellers or by contacting:

WestBow Press
A Division of Thomas Nelson & Zondervan
1663 Liberty Drive
Bloomington, IN 47403
www.westbowpress.com
1 (866) 928-1240

ISBN: 978-1-4908-2627-1 (sc)
ISBN: 978-1-4908-2628-8 (hc)
ISBN: 978-1-4908-2626-4 (e)

Library of Congress Control Number: 2014902689

Printed in the United States of America.

WestBow Press rev. date: 3/21/2014

I dedicate this book to Abba Father, my Keeper; Jesus Christ, my Best Friend and Savior, and to the Holy Spirit, who abides in me and gives me strength from day to day. Without You, Lord, I am nothing. Thank You, for loving me as I am and always seeing the best in me and for continuing to bring the best out of me.

{Let us boldly approach the Throne of Grace to obtain help in the time of trouble}

Hebrews 4:16

CONTENTS

PROLOGUE

The prayers of the righteous availeth much. God has called all of His children to pray; however, there are times when intense and bold prayers are needed for intense and exacting problems, and praying the Word is the answer. We are told that the Word of God is living and powerful and sharper than any double-edged sword (Hebrews 4:12). Praying the Word of God is effective because God told us that His Word would not return to Him void but would prosper in the purpose in which it was sent and accomplish its intended plan (Isaiah 55:11). How that's for a prayer target? Praying God's Word is effective because it always will hit the intended target. The prayers of this book were written to cover many areas in our lives. Since, we are often faced with many challenges and at times experience great spiritual assaults in various areas in our lives, families, marriages, ministries, etc., and the list goes on. The prayers in this book are fashioned to cover an expansive area and are to be prayed with confidence! Also, you should also feel free to include yourself in any of the prayers as impressed upon by the Holy Spirit, as they are written from an intercessor and prayer warrior viewpoint. Many of the prayers are written from the first person (because God wants us to pray for ourselves), second person (because we can entreat God to intervene on our and others' behalf), and third person (because God wants us to intercede for others). As intercessors and prayer warriors, God will often lead us to intercede and pray for numerous individuals simultaneously, so I made it easier by including all three forms in many of the prayers. Lastly, we are Christ's ambassadors. God is making His appeal through us. We are imploring others on the behalf of Christ to be reconciled to Christ (2 Corinthians 5:20; Genesis 18:22).

INTRODUCTION

The purpose of this prayer book is to help believers to effectively pray the Word of God. This book is about helping believers pray solution-based prayers and not problem-based prayers. God is a God of order, and we must pray His solution, which is His will, the Word. God exhorts us to call on Him, and He will answer us and show us great and mighty things we do not know (Jeremiah 33:3). God is a good God who loves us and loves to answer our prayers, especially when they are prayed in faith. God is pleased when we pray in faith. This is because faith is what unlocks the answers to our prayers and God is a rewarder of those who diligently seek Him (Hebrews 11:6). Furthermore, it takes faith to seek Him, and this is how we know that our prayers will be answered. God always answers our prayers when we pray according to His will, and God's Word is His will (1 John 5:14–15). Jesus prayed, "May Your Kingdom come and Your will be done on earth as it is in heaven," and as believers, God wants us to pray His will into the earth realm and His Word and faith is the key (Matthew 6:10). We are told in God's Word that He watches over His Word to perform it and that if we ask anything according to His will, knowing He hears us, He will give us the petition of our hearts (Isaiah 55:12; 1 John 5:15).

Praying the Word of God is His will. The Word of God is also considered the incorruptible seed of God, which means it will not die but live and produce fruit (1 Peter 1:23). The fruit that I am talking about is the answer to our prayers. Praying the Word causes changes in those who are being prayed for and the ones who are praying, this is because the Word is a double-edged sword. It is my belief that prayer is the currency of heaven and nothing happens in the life of a believer or on earth without first praying. Prayer is what changes things; it is a very powerful agent of change. Prayer has been known to stop divorces, discord, anger, jealousy, and a lot more. Prayer is a very effective arsenal used in stopping the forces of darkness (Mark 9:29) and will change people, families, marriages, destinies, communities, cultures and societies, nations, climates, companies, and industries. I was once told by an individual that no amount of praying, intercession, or fasting would help me, that it was a done deal for me. However, what that individual failed to realize was that prayer, intercession, and fasting was in fact the main and essential ingredient.

We are told in the Word of God, that the prayers of the righteous availeth much and that some things can only come out by prayer and fasting (James 5:16; Mark 9:29). We also know that God is not a man, that He should lie, nor the Son of Man that, He should repent (Numbers 23:19). God honors His Word above His name, and He has fidelity to His Word (Psalm 138:2). Also, we know what the Word of God says, that He watches over His Word to perform it and that His Word would not return void but would accomplish that which He sent it to do and that His Word is living and powerful and sharper than any double-edged sword (Isaiah 55:11; Hebrews 4:12). What this means is that whenever you pray the Word of God, you can expect God to answer your prayers. In the Old Testament God told His people to return to the altar with weeping and wailing and with fasting and praying (Joel

1:13–14; 2:12–13, 17). We are admonished in the Word of God to boldly approach the Throne of Grace to obtain help in the time of trouble, and that we should make intercessions, petitions, and supplications for the saints everywhere. We are to pray in the Spirit at all times and if My people who are called by My name will humble themselves and pray and seek My face, and turn from their wicked ways then will I hear from heaven and heal their land (Hebrews 4:16; Ephesians 6:18; 2 Chronicles 7:14). What the last Scripture means is that in order for our prayers to be effective, we need to confess our sins and obey God and only then will God answer our prayers.

King David, learned this principle early on in his career as God's anointed king, when he committed adultery with Bathsheba, which resulted in an unwanted pregnancy and the death of her husband, Uriah, at King David's hands (2 Samuel 11). King David, confessed his sin in Psalm 51. He admitted his guilt of adultery and crime of murder; he pleaded with God to blot out his transgressions and make him right with God again. We are instructed in the Word of God that He delights in the prayers of the righteous and that He will not despise the prayers of the destitute (Proverbs 15:8; Psalms 102:17).

Although, this book is about praying the Word of God, if you add penitence, praise and worship, fasting and intercession, I believe you will see excellent results. There are many examples in the Word of God in which His people—some very notable ones —sought God's help through penitence, prayer, intercession, fasting, praise and worship. God gave these individuals great and mighty victories, great miracles, great turnarounds, and great deliverance that altered the course of history. King David said, "This poor man cried out to the Lord and the Lord heard him and delivered him out of all of his fears" (Psalms 34:4). King David, was a man known to employ the weapons of praise and worship, prayer and fasting and as a result, God made him into a very powerful and very mighty king who was a priest and prophet. God even referred to him as a man after His own heart and that he served his generation and fulfilled his purpose (Acts 13:36). What an awesome testimony about King David, even after his failure with Bathsheba and the death of her husband, Uriah. It is my belief all of King David's, success was only possible through penitence, prayer, fasting, praise and worship. King Jehoshaphat and King Hezekiah both cried out to God when opposing enemy forces threatened to annihilate them and their kingdoms. God in return delivered them both with His awesome power that sent shockwaves throughout both enemy army ranks and cause both kings to gain the total victory because God fought for both of them (2 Chronicles 20:1–29; Isaiah 36, 37).

"Why?" you may ask. Because they turned to Him for help in the form of penitence, prayer and fasting, intercession, praise and worship. The most incredible part about these two kings was that they never had to lift a finger because God fought for them and let them see the awesome defeat of their enemies (2 Chronicles 20:19–23;Isaiah 37:33–38). Queen Esther was a very powerful and very influential woman of God who was brought to the palace by God for such a time as this in order, to save her people from total annihilation from Haman's plot. She was also a very powerful intercessor along with her cousin Mordecai, who with her court employed the weapons of prayer, intercession, and fasting to reverse and turn back Haman's plot to totally annihilate the whole Jewish race and caused Haman's and his ten sons to die instead of them along with a host of others who were in alignment with Haman's destructive plot (Esther 2:17; 3:4–15; 4: 1–16; 5:1–7; 7:1–10; 8:3–16; 9:5–13). The decision was totally eradicated.

In turn, the Jews were able to pursue their enemies until none were left in place of the original death edict (Esther 9:15–16). Purim was decreed in its place and is still celebrated by the children of Israel to this very day, but it was birth only through prayer, fasting, and intercession (Esther 9:19–32). God did exceedingly and abundantly above that which they could ever ask, hope, wish, or pray (Ephesians 3:20). The most amazing thing was that they were only seeking and praying for their lives to be spared (Esther 4:1, 15–16), but God in His loving kindness did what they could not do (Esther 9:1–6, 15–16). God showed up and showed out on their behalf. Paul and Silas were delivered out of prison at midnight when they began to sing, pray, and worship, and God's glory filled the prison cell and caused an earthquake that shook loose all the chains and prison doors, which resulted in all the prisoners being set free. It even set the jailer free from the prison of sin along with his whole entire household. What is so remarkable about Paul and Silas prayer was that God answered not only to free them but to free the other prisoners as well (Acts 16:25–34). The Apostle Peter also was freed from jail because of the saints who were fervently praying for him in the Upper Room. God caused the prison guards who were guarding Peter's prison cell to become completely oblivious to his divine deliverance, while an Angel of the Lord freed him from prison all because of the fervent prayers of the saints in the Upper Room and The Angel of the Lord then led Peter to safety (Acts 12:5-12). When Peter showed up at their door, they were still travailing for Peter and could not believe Peter was at their door (Acts 12:12–16). This was because they were so heavily travailing for Peter through intercession that they did not realize that God went ahead and answered their prayers (Isaiah 65:24). This is a prime example of the prayers of the righteous availing much.

This is the kind of power you and I both have when we pray in faith believing that God will answer our petitions, requests, and supplications. Jonah, is another example of how prayer changes destinies. He was told by God to go to Nineveh and warn the people of their evil. Instead, Jonah rebelled and went down to Joppa by boat, and a great storm arose. He was then thrown off the boat he was on, and God prepared a large fish that swallowed him whole. Jonah's only way out of the fish was through praying, praising, and honoring his vow to obey God by going to Nineveh (Jonah 1:1–17; 2:1–9). So prayer also brings personal deliverance from rebellion, willfulness, and poor choices. These are just a few examples of how God delivers His people through the use of penitence, prayer, intercession, fasting, praise and worship. Penitence, prayer, intercession, fasting, praise and worship are effective in breaking down strongholds, casting down vain imaginations, and bringing disobedient thoughts into the obedience of Jesus Christ (2 Corinthians 10:4).

Whenever you engage the Enemy, you always start with praise and worship because God inhabits the praises of His people and worship causes God to fight on your behalf (Psalm 22:3; 2 Chronicles 20:21). So, when you begin with praise and worship, God's presence will show up, and He will fight on your behalf. When you add God's Word coupled with prayer, it's like a hammer that breaks the rocks into pieces (2 Chronicles 20:23; Isaiah 55:11; 2 Corinthians 10:4–5; Jeremiah 5:14; 1:9; Zechariah 1:6; Jeremiah 23:29). Now, you have the formula for great prayer and breakthrough.

Prayer will change the stoniest of hearts and make them tender and responsive and obedient (Ezekiel 36:26–27, 37–38). Praying God's Word will deliver individuals from Satan's influence and demonic oppression and demonic suggestion, and will fill them with the Holy Spirit, thus causing them to will and to do God's perfect pleasure––will give them the very mind of Christ (James 4:2,5,6; 5:13–17; John 14:16; Philippians 2:13; 1 Corinthians 2:16). Let's go to God's Throne of Grace now.

CHAPTER ONE

BACKSLIDER

The heart of the Father is love and reconciliation. We are told in the Word of God that God is still married to the backslider and has fidelity to His Word (Jeremiah 3:14; Psalms 138:2). The heart of the Father is to seek and save the lost. Remember the parable that Jesus spoke about the lost sheep that wandered away from the flock in the Gospel of Matthew 18:12–14? The shepherd left the other ninety-nine sheep in order to find the one lost sheep. The Father's heart can be illustrated in the parable about the "Prodigal Son" in the Gospel of Luke 15:11–32. The son asked his father for his inheritance early, and the father gave it to him. The son then took his inheritance and went down to a far country and spent it on riotous living and prostitutes. When he spent all his inheritance, he found himself working in a pigpen and feeding pigs. He was hungry and without food to eat. And when he came to himself, he said, "At my father's house there is food to eat and even the servants have bread. I will go at once back to my father's house and beg for mercy and to become a servant." So, the son returned back to his father's house, and when the father saw his son from afar, he ran and embraced him. And the Prodigal Son proceeded to tell his father,

"I am your servant." But the father only thought of him as his own son. The father then called all his servants to bring the best robe and kill the fatted calf and prepare a feast for his son. "My son, who was once dead, is now alive," and this is the heart of our Heavenly Father toward all of His children. He is not wanting that anyone should perish, but that all come to repentance (2 Peter 3:9).

PRAYER FOR BACKSLIDERS

Lord, I pray that You would bring name(s), who strayed from You, back into his/her/their own borders and out of the land of his/her/their captivity. You are married to the backsliders, and You said, "I have seen his/her/their ways, but I will heal him/he/ them." I will guide him/her/them and restore comfort to him/her/them and help him/her/them to mourn and confess his/her/their sins. You have said, You, gladly instruct those who have gone astray for the sake of Your name O' Lord, forgive his/her/their iniquity, though it is great. Turn to him/her/them because he/she/they (is/are) lonely and afflicted. May he/she/they say, "The troubles of my heart have multiplied and my distress, please, take away all my sins." May he/she/they say, "After I strayed, I repented after I came to understand, I beat my breast. I was ashamed and humiliated because I bored the disgrace of my youth." Lord, You said, "That godly sorrow leads to repentance." Bring him/her/them back into right fellowship with You. In Jesus' name, amen (Jeremiah 31:16–17, Jeremiah 3:14, Isaiah 57:18; Psalms 25:8, 11, 16–18; Jeremiah 31:18-19, 2 Corinthians 7:10).

CHAPTER TWO

ANGER AND REBELLION

Anger and bitterness are often the reason behind rebellion. King David's son Absalom was a prime example of how, when anger is inappropriately dealt with, it often circumvents a person's life, family, marriage, career, etc., the list goes on and on (2 Samuel 13:20–29). It creates seeds of bitterness that when the seeds sprout up produces the fruit of rebellion. Rebellion is simply anger improperly dealt with. A rebellious person often says to him or herself that "I was wronged, but I did not receive the just recompense. My cry fell on deaf ears, so I will take matters into my own hands until I receive the just recompense that I deserve" (2 Samuel 14:28–33). "I will not listen to anyone else because no one can help me." Rebellion is simply perverted justice. Instead of waiting on God or authority figures to handle the injustice, the rebellious says, "I will handle it with my own plan." This is often to his or her detriment.

Absalom was angry that his brother Annan had raped his sister Tamara, and when he brought the matter to his father's attention, King David did not handle the matter well; he only became very angry (2 Samuel 13:21). This in turn caused Absalom to take matters into his own hands, which led to his killing his half -brother Annan and to an insurrection against his father's kingdom (2 Samuel 13:22–39; 15:1–37). Absalom's refusal to repent from rebellion and anger led to his ultimate demise (2 Samuel 18:9). This can happen to anyone if anger is left uncheck and is allowed to fester and grow into rebellion. That's why it is very important to pray for those we know who have a problem with anger or to pray for ourselves when we become angry. God will listen, deliver, and give us direction.

PRAYER AGAINST ANGER

Lord, You, said, "That in our anger do not sin, do not let the sun go down on your anger, but get over it quickly because when you are angry, you give a mighty foothold to the devil; and that anger rests in the bosom of a fool." You also, said that we should be slow to anger and slow to speak, quick to listen, and to forgive because anger does not allow for us to be righteous as You want us to be. May name(s) be given the revelatory knowledge and understanding about the importance of letting go of anger. May name(s) refrain from anger and turn from wrath because it only leads to evil and harm. Where name(s) has/have allowed anger and his/her/their (life/lives), may he/she/they repent and confess it as sin because you said, "An angry man (woman) stirs up dissension, and that a hot-tempered one commits many sins and that a fool gives full vent to his (her) anger, but a wise person keeps himself (herself) under control; mockers stir up a city but wise men (women) turn away from anger." Enable name(s) to get rid of all bitterness, rage and anger, brawling and slander, along with every form of malice. Instead, be kind and compassionate to one another, forgiving each other, just as Christ in God for gave you. May name(s) understand that he/she/they must rid himself/herself/themselves from such things as well as filthy language from his/her/their lip(s). May name(s) put on the new self, which is being renewed in the knowledge in the image of its Creator. Clothe yourself with compassion, kindness, humility, gentleness, and patience. Bear with each other and forgive whatever grievances you may have against one another. Forgive as the Lord forgave you. And over all these virtues, put on love, which binds them all together in perfect unity. Let the peace of Christ rule in your hearts since as members of one body you were called to peace and be thankful. Let the Word of Christ dwell in you richly as you teach and admonish one another with all wisdom and as you sing psalms, hymns, and spiritual songs with gratitude in your hearts to God. And whatever you do, whether in word or deed, do it all in the name of the Lord Jesus Christ, giving thanks to God the Father through Him. May name(s) be given the understanding that love is not easily angered and may he/she/they not avenge himself/herself/themselves but rather give vengeance to God because You said, "Vengeance is Mine. I will repay those that deserve it." In Jesus' name, amen. (Ephesians 4:26–27; Ecclesiastes 7:9; James 1:19–20; Psalms 37:8; Proverbs 29:22; Proverbs 15:18, Proverbs 29:11; Ephesians 4:31-32; Colossians 3:8, 10, 12–17; 1Corinthians 13:5; Romans 12:19).

PRAYER AGAINST REBELLION

Lord, may <u>name of person(s)</u> come to see his/her/their rebellion as the sin of witchcraft. The rebellious live in a sun-scorched land. He does not reward the wicked with His blessings; He gives them their full share of punishment. An evil man (woman) is bent only on rebellion; a merciless official will be sent against him/her/them. Sometimes mere words are not enough—discipline is needed. For the words may not be heeded. So he/she/they will sit in deepest gloom, prisoner(s) suffering in iron chains, for he/she/they had rebelled against the words of God and despise the counsel of the Most High. So He subjected them to bitter labor; they stumbled, and there was no one to help. They were bound in chains, held fast by cords of affliction, He tells them what they have done, that they have sinned arrogantly. He takes the trouble to point out to them the reason, what they have done wrong, or how they have behaved proudly. He delivers by distresses! This makes them listen to Him. He makes them listen to correction and commands them to repent of their evil. A man (woman) who refuses to admit his/her mistakes can never be successful. But if he/she/they confess the mistakes, he/she/they will get another chance. If he/she/they obey and served Him, he/she/they will spend the rest of his/her/their days in prosperity and his/her/ their years in contentment. But if he/she/they do not listen, he/she/ they will perish by the sword. But if you stop your sinning and start obeying the Lord your God, He will cancel all the punishment He announced against you. "Let your remorse tear at hearts and not your garments." Return to the Lord your God, for He is gracious and merciful. He is not easily angered; He is full of kindness,

9

and not anxious to punish you. In Jesus' name, amen (1 Samuel 15:23; Psalms 68:6, Proverb 17:11, Proverbs 29:19; Job 36:6, Psalms 107:10-12; Job 36: 8–9; 36:15; 36:10, Proverbs 28:13, Job 36:11-12, Jeremiah 26:13; Joel 2:13).

CHAPTER THREE

DELIVERANCE FROM PRIDE AND THE DECEPTION OF PRIDE

Pride can be summed up in the overestimation of one's self-worth. It's arrogance in the purest form. It is a very great sin. It's the very sin that led to Satan being kicked out of heaven. In Luke 10:18, Jesus told His disciples, "Behold, I seen Satan fall like lightning from heaven," and in Isaiah 14:12, speaks about his down fall. "How you are fallen from heaven, O' Lucifer, son of the morning! How are you cut down to the ground." Why was he cut down to the ground? He said, to himself "I will ascend to heaven and rule the angels. I will take the highest throne. I will preside on the Mount of Assembly far away in the north. I will climb to the highest heavens and be like the Most High." But instead, he was brought down to the pit of hell, down to the lowest depths (Isaiah 14:12–15). You may ask, "What brought about his overestimation of self-worth?" His chief position as anointed guardian cherub, his access to the holy mountain of God, and his being able to walk among the stones of fire. Another contributing factor was he was created in perfection of wisdom and beauty. He was the emblem of beauty because he was clothed in precious gemstones of every kind (see Ezekiel 28:12–13). He was perfect in every way until sin was found in him because of his great wealth, beauty, and wisdom. His heart became filled with pride because of his beauty, and he corrupted his wisdom because of his splendor. As a direct result, he was cast to the ground (see Ezekiel 28:12–18). He was lifted up in pride due to his wisdom and beauty.

Pride is a sin that God detests, and we are told in the Word of God how the proud will not go unpunished (Proverbs 6:16–19; 16:5; 21:24; 29:23). That's because it's a gross misrepresentation of one's self-worth. There are many tragic examples of individuals in the Word of God who fell victim to pride—Nabal of Carmel, husband of Abigail (see 1 Samuel 25:2–11, 36–38), King Nebuchadnezzar(see Daniel 4:4–37),King Belshazzar(see Daniel 5:1–30), and Sennacherib, King of Assyria (see Isaiah 36:4–20; 37: 4-38), just to name a few. Pride will cause you to lose the good things that you once had (Proverbs 2:22) because it is a corruptor and blinder of reality. It creates self-delusions of one's self-worth and self-importance (Proverbs 25:27; Galatians 6:3, Proverbs 21:30, Proverbs 13:19, Proverbs 11:28). Pride has caused many bright and promising individuals with budding careers, great wealth, and great power to be cut short and has resulted in their losing it all– success and prosperity. Pride will also greatly impact those closest to the individual infected by this insidious sin. That's why God warns us that He opposes the proud but gives grace to the humble (James 4:6). Nothing ruins more lives, marriages, families, careers, etc., than the sin of pride (1 Samuel 3:11–14; 4:1–22; 2 Kings 19:22; 2 Chronicles 26:16). Why? Because a person overtaken by pride replaces God with the god of self and the worship of self (Psalms 10:4; 73:9; Jeremiah 49:16).

A prideful person is self-centered and self-absorbed (2 Corinthians 10:12; 2 Timothy 3:2; Jeremiah 9:23; Romans 1:22). The proud rarely have time for others (spouses, family, etc.) because self is on the throne. They are also very arrogant, puffed-up, haughty, mockers of God, use perverse speech, and are self-conceited (Proverbs 21:24; Isaiah 2:11, 17). They often act in very foolish and sinful ways (Job 20:6, Proverbs 14:3; Psalms 31:18; Psalms 73:6, Psalms 59:12). They are often self-taught and refuse all advice, discipline, and correction (Isaiah 50:11; Proverbs 12:15; 15:12). They often think *only I am right, and everyone else is wrong*. These people often make unrealistic demands on others but will not allow others to do likewise to them (e.g., King Nebuchadnezzar Daniel 2:1–13). They have a follow the leader complex and are never happy unless others do as they say. Lastly, God wants His people to be humble because it allows God to bless, help, promote, honor, prosper, and impart wisdom as well as grace (Proverbs 15:33; Job 5:11). When we are humble, God can teach and correct us too (Proverbs 13:1; 9:8).

PRAYER FOR THE DELIVERANCE FROM PRIDE

Lord, You said that You oppose the proud but give grace to the humble. May You give revelatory knowledge and wisdom to name(s) today that when pride comes, then comes disgrace and pride goes before the downfall and that a man's (woman's) pride brings him (her) low and all the peoples of the earth are regarded as nothing. He does as He pleases with the powers of heaven and the people of the earth. No one can hold back His hand or say to Him, "What have You done?" May name(s) say as Nebuchadnezzar, "Now I praise and exalt and glorify the King of Heaven, because everything He does is right in all His ways are just in those who walk in pride He is able to humble." Therefore, names(s) be pleased to accept my advice: Renounce your sins by doing what is right, and your wickedness by being kind to the oppressed. It may be then that your prosperity will continue. The decision is announced by the messengers the holy ones declared the verdict so that the living may know that the Most High is sovereign over the kingdoms of men and gives to them anyone He wished and sets over them the lowliest of men. May name(s) be given the understanding that humility brings wisdom and precedes honor and that a man (woman) of lowly spirit gains honor. So I ask, Lord, that You allow name(s) to see the value of having a humble heart and may he/she/they humbled himself/herself/ themselves before the Lord so that You can lift him/her/them up. In Jesus' name, amen (James 4:6, Proverbs 11:2; 18:12, Proverbs 29:23, Daniel 4:35, 37, Daniel 4:27, Daniel 4:35, Proverbs 15:33, Proverbs 29:23, James 4:10).

PRAYER FOR DELIVERANCE FROM THE DECEPTION OF PRIDE

The Lord says: let not the wise men (women) bask in his (her) wisdom, nor the mighty man (woman) in his (her) might, nor the rich man (woman) in his/her riches. Let them boast in this alone that they truly know Me, understand that I am the Lord of justice and of righteousness whose love is steadfast; and that I love to be this way." Pride goes before destruction and haughtiness before a fall. Before every man (woman) there lies a wide and Pleasant Road he (she) thinks is right but the end is death. Pride disgusts the Lord. Take my word for it - proud men (women) shall be punished. Humility and reverence for the Lord will make you both wise and honored. Proud men (women) end in shame, but the meek become wise. May he/she/they not be wise in his/her/their own eyes but rather repent and turn from evil. May he/she/ they be given the common sense to stay away from evil persons and learn to walk in God's ways. May (name(s) incline his/her/their ears to wisdom and his/her/their heart(s) to understanding and walk before You humbly. May he/she/they be delivered from every evil work and preserved for Your Heavenly Kingdom. And lastly may wisdom and truth enter the very center of his/her/their being(s), filling his/her/their life (lives) with joy. In Jesus' powerful name, amen (Jeremiah 9:23–24, Proverbs 16:18; Proverbs 16:25, Proverbs 16:5, Proverbs 15:33, Proverbs 11:2, Proverbs 3:7, Proverbs 2:11, Proverbs 2:2, Micah 6:8; 2 Timothy 4:18, Proverbs 2:10).

CHAPTER FOUR

GODLY WISDOM RATHER THAN EARTHLY WISDOM

God wants His people to have wisdom and to become wise, but He doesn't want them following the world's way of acquiring wisdom or becoming wise. The world's wisdom is gained through shrewdness and the use of deception, craftiness, and selfish ambition (James 3:14–16). This can be illustrated in the Gospel of Luke 16:1–13 in Jesus' parable of the "Shrewd Manager." The shrewd manager worked for a very rich man from whom he was stealing, and when the rich man found out, he called the manager to fire him. So the shrewd manager, knowing he would be fired, strategized and came up with a plan to save face. He contacted each of his boss's debtors and made a deal with each of them in order to win their friendship and to ensure he would have a place to live after he was terminated. He asked each client how much they owed his boss. One said, "A hundred gallons of olive oil," so he told the debtor to slash the bill to fifty gallons of olive oil. The next person said, "He owes a hundred bushels of wheat," so the manager told that client to slash his bill to eighty bushels of wheat. Afterward his boss commended the shrewd manager for his cunning self-preservation. Jesus, then remarked how the people in this world are shrewder than those who belong to the kingdom of light when dealing with the world affairs (in his case, buying friendship by dishonest means). But Jesus, commented that those who buy friendship through dishonest means will not be admitted into heaven, but into hell. We are told throughout God's Word, particularly in the book of Job, that God uses the wisdom of the wise against them and frustrates their plans. Why does God do this? Because it's not His wisdom and this kind of wisdom is earthly, sensual meaning only appealing to the natural senses, cunning, deceptive, based on self-ambitions, based on human philosophy, and demonic in origin (James 3:15). It has no roots in God.

In 1 Corinthians 1:25, we are told that God uses the foolish things of this world to confound the wise and that even the wisest of plans or most brilliant of plans He ignores. The kind of wisdom God wants for His children is found in James 3:13, 17. We are told that when we are wise, we will live lives of steady goodness, so only our good deeds will pour forth, and if we don't brag about them, then we will be truly wise. Wisdom that comes from heaven is also pure and full of quiet gentleness. Then it is peace-loving and courteous. It allows discussion and is willing to yield to others; it is full of mercy and good. It is wholehearted and straightforward and sincere. We are also told in Job 28 that even with all the advancement of men and human ability to excavate the earth depths in order to extract the hidden treasures that God deposited in the earth and then being able to afford them will not give you wisdom. But in verses 22, 23, 27, and 28, we are told how "Destruction and Death speaks of knowing something about it. God knows where to find it and will declare it to all who will listen. He established it and examined it thoroughly. And this is what he says to all mankind: Look, to fear the Lord is true wisdom; to shun evil is true understanding. Also, see how in Proverbs 1:7 and Psalms 111:10 respectably, how men become wise is through trust and reverence for God. Growth in wisdom comes from obeying God's Word. If you look in Psalms 112:1–4, 9, you will see how the psalmist encourages us to praise the Lord, because all who fear God and trust in Him are bless beyond expression. And happy is the man who delights in doing His commands because his children will be honored everywhere, for good men's sons have a special heritage. He himself shall be wealthy, and his good deeds will never be forgotten. He is kind and merciful. He gives generously to those in need. His good deeds will never be forgotten. He shall have influence and honor.

Now contrast the "Godly Man" with the "Shrewd Manager," who was dishonest and a thief. He was self-centered, and he only thought about how he could meet his own needs through craftiness and trickery with the hopes of winning favor through cheating. Now had the "Shrewd Manager," applied godly wisdom, he would not have had the fear of losing his job because wisdom would have preserved him and he would have instead received promotion and honor from God. He would have had a permanent home, instead of fearing where he would stay after being fired. He would of have had true friendship without compromise. He would have had favor on the job, which would have had made him a very valuable employee. So to sum it up as described in Psalms 112, living by godly wisdom leads others to receive good results. The "Shrewd Manager" lived by earthly wisdom; whereas, the "Godly Man" in Psalms 112 lived by godly wisdom.

PRAYER FOR GODLY WISDOM
RATHER THAN EARTHLY

I thank You, Heavenly Father, that the weapons of our warfare are not carnal but mighty in God for the pulling down of strongholds, casting down vain imaginations that exalt itself against the true knowledge of God and bringing every disobedient thoughts into the captivity of Christ Jesus. Father, You said, that You have given us the keys to the Kingdom of Heaven and that whatever we bind on earth is already bound in heaven. So I (we) bind spiritual deception and earthly wisdom, which is unspiritual, inspired by the devil in the person(s) being prayed for. It is cunning and crafty steeped in deception and human philosophy, it is full of jealousy and selfish ambition, which is tainted with disorder and every kind of evil. But I (we) loose in name of person(s) the wisdom that comes from Heaven, which is first pure and full of quiet gentleness. Then it is peace-loving and courteous. It allows discussion and is willing to yield to others; it is full of mercy and good deeds. It is wholehearted and straightforward and sincere. And those who are peacemakers will plant seeds of peace and reap a harvest of goodness. The fear of God is the beginning of wisdom and how can men (women) be wise? The only way to begin is by reverence for God. For growth in wisdom comes from obeying His laws. For the value of wisdom is far above rubies; nothing can be compared with it. Wisdom and good judgment live together for wisdom knows where to discover knowledge and understanding. If anyone respects and fears God, he/she/they will hate evil. For wisdom hates pride, arrogance, corruption and deceit of every kind. I wisdom give good advice and common sense. Those who search for me shall surely find me. Unending riches, honor, justice, and righteousness are mine to distribute. My gifts are better than precious gold or sterling silver! My paths are those of justice and righteousness! Listen to me! For I have important information for everything I say is right and true, for I hate lies and every kind of deception. My advice is wholesome and good. There is nothing of evil in it. My words are plain and clear to anyone with a half a mind—if it is only open! My instruction is far more valuable than silver and gold. I love all who love me. Those who love and follow me are indeed wealthy. I fill their treasuries. God opposes the proud but gives grace to the humble. So don't be proud of following the wisdom of this world. For the wisdom of this world is foolishness to God. As it says in the book of Job God uses man's own brilliance to trap him; he stumbles over his own wisdom and falls. And again in the book of Psalms, we are told that the Lord knows full well how the human mind reasons and how foolish and futile it is. Don't be conceited, sure of your own wisdom. Instead, trust and reverence the Lord and turn your back on evil; when you do that, then you will be given renewed health and vitality. Have two goals: wisdom—that is, knowing and doing right—and common sense. Don't let them slip away, for they will fill you with living energy, and are a feather in your cap. They will keep you safe from defeat and disaster and from stumbling off the trail. For the Lord grants wisdom! His every word is a treasure of knowledge and understanding. He grants good sense to the godly—His saints. Thank You, for granting <u>name(s) of person(s)</u> with good sense. Thank You, for being <u>name(s) of person(s)</u>' shield, protecting and guarding his/her/their pathway. I (we) ask that You show him/her/them how to distinguish right from wrong, how to find the right decision every time, so that wisdom and truth will entered the very center of his/her/their being, filling <u>name(s) of person(s)</u>' life(lives) with joy. I (we) ask that he/she/ they will be given the sense to stay away from evil men.

Only wisdom from the Lord can save a man (woman) from the flattery of prostitutes. So follow the steps of the godly instead, and stay on the right path, for only good men (women) enjoy life to the full, evil men (women) lose the good things they might have had, and they themselves shall be destroyed. Never forget to be truthful and kind. Hold these virtues tightly. The curse of God is on the wicked, but His blessing is on the upright. The wise are promoted to honor, but fools are promoted to shame. And Lord, I (we) want name(s) of person(s) to be wise and promoted to honor and not shame. In Jesus' name, amen (2 Corinthians 10:4-5; Matthew 16:19, James 3:15-18; Proverbs 9:10; Psalms 111:10, Proverbs 8:11-14, 8:17-20;Proverbs 8:6-10; Proverbs 8:21; James 4:6; 1 Corinthians 3:21, 1 Corinthians 3:19-22, Proverbs 3:7-8, Proverbs 3:21-23, Proverbs 2:6-11, Proverbs 3:16, Proverbs 3:20-22, Proverbs 3:3, Proverbs 3:33, Proverbs 3:35).

CHAPTER FIVE

CORRUPTING COMMUNICATION AND SPEECH SEASONED WITH GRACE

We live in a world where four-letter epithets, abusive language, lying and complaining are very ubiquitous, and sadly many who professed to be born-again Christians use corrupting speech. We are told in the Word of God that we live in this world but are not of this world (John 17:14). Many Christians confuse the two. Many professing born-again Christians believe that in order to be relevant in today's culture, they need to speak as the world does. However, nowhere in the Word of God does it say we as believers need to assimilate to the world's way of speaking. In fact, we are expected to do the opposite. God desires that we as His followers use wholesome, edifying and encouraging, uplifting and faith-filled speech that moves mountains and break rocks into pieces (Colossians 4:6; Ephesians 4:29; 1 Thessalonians 5:11; Mark

11:13–14, 20–23; Jeremiah 23:29). Our speech should be faith-filled so that we can minister life to others and to the dying world around us (Romans 4:17; Proverbs 18:20). Our speech needs to be the kind that instructs other believers on how to live victorious lives (Philippians 4:13; Colossians 1:29; Romans 5:17). We are admonished in the Word of God that for every idle word we speak, we will have to give an account on The Day of Judgment (Matthew 12:36), and if that's not scary enough, we are told that we will be either justified or condemned by our words (Matthew 12:37).

That's very sobering to think about, huh? You may ask, "Why?" Because we sin by what we say (James 3:6; Matthew 12:35; Matthew 15:11, Psalms 10:7; 12:2; Psalms 52:2–4). If you speak doubt, it is sin because it's not from faith (Numbers 13:31–32; 14:1–11; Romans 14:23). I bet this makes you want to take stock of what you say and start using speech that's seasoned with grace. How do you develop speech that's seasoned with grace? By cultivating a heart of gratitude (Philippians 4:8). How does one cultivate a heart of gratitude? By developing a life of thanksgiving to God (Psalms 34:1–3), worshipping Him (Psalms 96:9), praying and thanking Him for each answer (Philippians 4:6), fellowshipping with other thankful believers (Colossians 3:14–16), studying the Word of God with other believers (Acts 17:11), making a joyful noise unto the Lord (Psalms 98:4; Psalms 33:3; Psalms 100:1; Psalms 47:1-5; Psalms 66:1,4) singing Psalms, hymns, and spiritual songs (Ephesians 5:19).

PRAYER OF DELIVERANCE FROM CORRUPTING COMMUNICATION

Lord, may name(s) avoid godless chatter because those who indulge in it will become more and more ungodly; let no corrupt talk come out of your mouth. Let only that which is necessary for edification, so that those who listen will be blessed. For every idle word people may speak, they will have to give an account on the Day of Judgment. If you want a longer, fruitful life, keep your mouth from deceit and your mouth from speaking evil. Let your speech be seasoned with grace. Therefore encourage each other with these words. Put on the Lord Jesus Christ and make no provision for the flesh to fulfill its lust, speak to one another in love. Let the Word of Christ dwell in you richly as you teach and admonish one another with all wisdom and as you sing Psalms, hymns, and spiritual songs with gratitude in your hearts to God. And whatever you do, whether in word or deed, do it all in the name of the Lord Jesus, giving thanks to God the Father through Him. But now you must rid yourselves of all such things as these: anger, rage, malice, slander and filthy language from your lips. Do not lie to each other since you have taken off your old self with its practices nor should there be any obscenity, foolish talk, or course joking which are out of place, but rather thanksgiving. Let the peace of Christ rule in your heart, since as members of one body you were called to peace so be thankful. Turn away from godless chatter and opposing ideas of what is falsely called knowledge, which some have professed and in so doing have wandered from the faith see to it that no one takes you captive through hollow and deceptive philosophy, which depends on human tradition and the basic principles of this world rather than on Christ. Nevertheless, God's solid foundation stands firm, sealed with this inscription: the Lord knows those who are His, and everyone who confesses the name of the Lord must turn away from wickedness. In Jesus' name, amen (2 Timothy 2:16, Ephesians 4:29, Matthew 12:36, Psalms 34:12–13, Colossians 4:6; 1 Thessalonians 4:18, Romans 13:14, Colossians 3:16-17, Colossians 3:8-9, Ephesians 5:4, Colossians 3:15, 1Timothy 6:20-21, 2 Timothy 2:19).

PRAYER FOR SPEECH SEASONED WITH GRACE

Dear Heavenly Father, I thank You that name of person(s)' speech is season with grace so when he/she/they speaks, it edifies those that are listening. He/she/they is (are) slow to anger and slow to speak and quick to listen. He/she/they make no provision for the flesh because he/she/they have put on the Lord Jesus Christ. He/she/they does not (do not) act rudely or uncomely, nor does he/she/they demand his/her/their own way. Thank You that, he/she/they has (have) the law of kindness on his/her/their tongue(s) and he/she/they open his/her/their mouth(s) with wisdom. I thank You that he/her/their gentleness is evident to everyone because You said a soft answer turns away wrath but harsh words cause quarrels. Gentle words cause life and health; gripping brings discouragement. The upright speak what is helpful; the wicked speak rebellion. Evil words destroy. Godly skill rebuilds. And I (we) thank You that he/she/they speak only kind words that are like honey, which are enjoyable and helpful to others and also encouraging. In Jesus' name, amen (Colossians 4:6; Ephesians 4:29; James 1:19; Romans 13:14; 1 Corinthians 13:5; Proverbs 31:26; Philippians 4:5; Proverbs 15:1, Proverbs 15:4; Proverbs 10:32, Proverbs 11:9, Proverbs 16:24).

CHAPTER SIX

THOSE WHOSE HEARTS ARE HARDENED TO SIN

The way of the transgressor is hard (Proverbs 13:15). This is because their hearts are only bent on evil, and when people's hearts are bent on evil, they live by their vain imaginations (Genesis 6:5). Their hearts are hardened to God, and they are ignorant to His ways (Romans 1:28). We are told in the book of Proverbs that without restraints the people run wild (Proverbs 29:18). This is very indicative of the world today. People live without restraint. As a result, they live according to the darkness of their hearts (Jude 1:18–19). But, God wants to penetrate this darkness with the light of His truth (Colossians 1:13; 2 Timothy 3:16). This is because a life hardened to God will only produce death and eventual eternal destruction (Galatians 6:8a; Romans 6:23; 8:6; Matthew 25:46). God is a God of love, and He does not delight in the death of the wicked (Ephesians 2:4; Ezekiel 18:23). He desires that all people be saved and come to repentance (1 Timothy 2:4). Hell was never created for anyone; it was created originally for Satan and his angels. However, those who do go to hell are there by their own free admission (Ezekiel 33:11; 2

Peter 3:9; Matthew 25:41; Revelation 20:10). God gives everyone the opportunity to come to repentance (1 Timothy 2:4). That's why we must stand in the gap through prayers for our spouses, families, loved ones, neighbors, and co-workers. We could be the very ones God uses to snatch their very lives from the flames (Jude 1:23–24). We need to ask God to give them tender hearts that are responsive to the things of God, and we must ask for God to break up the fallow ground of their hearts (Ezekiel 36:26; Hosea 10:12) so their hearts and minds will be opened to the things of God (John 6:44; 12:32). God can melt the heart of stone.

All throughout the Old Testament His people's hearts were hardened to the sin of idolatry, and time and time again He pleaded with them to return back to Him. Often, they refused to return to Him, and this led to God sending judgment and exile to correct and discipline them (Jeremiah 18:12–18; 19:3–15). Then they would repent and follow Him wholeheartedly for a little while, and then they would return to the sin of idolatry (Hosea 14). This was not true repentance. God desires true repentance in which there is a permanent change of hearts and perspectives (Joel 2:13; Jonah 3:4–10). He also desires that we follow after Him wholeheartedly, and He promises to help us follow after Him wholeheartedly (Jeremiah 29:12–13; 31:31–34; 32:39–40). Lastly, He promises that He would instruct transgressors in His ways and gladly teach those who have strayed from the proper paths (Psalms 25:8).

PRAYER FOR THOSE WHOSE HEARTS ARE HARDENED TO SIN

Lord, You said that we can boldly approach Your throne of grace to obtain help in our time of need. We come on the behalf of our loved one(s). Lord, Your Word says that which is impossible for me (us) is possible with You, so I (we) ask that You deliver loved one(s) from having a sinful, unbelieving heart that turns away from You O' God and also, from the deceitfulness of sin. Lord, please deliver him/her/them from stubbornness, hard-heartedness, lack of remorse, lack of repentance, adultery, lying, stealing, pride, anger, bitterness, cheating, jealousy, envy, selfishness, abuse, unforgiveness, lack of reverence for the things of God, impurity, sexual immorality, hatred, (or anything you see exhibited in your loved one(s). God, we know that You, in justice will punish anyone who does such things as these. May they realize that Your patience with them is so, that they can repent. But You will terribly punish those who fight against the truth of God and walk in evil ways –God's anger will be poured out upon them; if you do not repent and so you will be saving up terrible punishment for yourselves because of your stubbornness in refusing to turn from your sin. For there is coming a day of wrath when God will be the just judge of all the world. He will give each one whatever his/her/their deeds deserve. He will give eternal life to those who patiently do the will of God, seeking for the unseen glory and honor and eternal life that He offers. An evil person is stubborn, but a godly person will reconsider. May loved one(s) reconsider his/her/their ways. A person can justify their every deeds but God looks at their motives. God is more pleased when we are just and fair then when we give Him gifts. Do not be deceived: God is not mocked, for whatsoever you sow, you will also reap, so repent so that times of refreshing may begin and so your transgressions may be blotted out. Keep my <u>loved one(s)</u> from willful sins; may they not rule over <u>loved one(s)</u>. Then my (our) <u>loved one(s)</u> will be blameless, innocent of great transgression. Iniquity is atoned for by mercy and truth; evil is avoided by reverence for God. Fill his/her/their heart(s) with praise and obedience to Your will and Your way because it is Your Spirit inside of him/her/them that causes him/her/them to will and do Your perfect pleasure. In Jesus' name, amen (Hebrews 4:16; Luke 18:27; Hebrews 3:12-13, Romans 2:2–4, Romans 2:8; Romans 2:5-7, Proverbs 21:29; Proverbs 21:2-3, Galatians 6:7; Acts 3:19; Psalms 51:1; Psalms 19:13, Proverbs 16:6, Philippians 2:13).

CHAPTER SEVEN

HOPE FOR THE DELIVERANCE AND REPENTANCE OF LOVED ONES

Many times when we are standing in the gap in prayer for loved ones who are in bondage to sin or overtaken by a fault, we can become tired and discouraged because other people (Mark 5:35–41) and the enemy of our souls are constantly shooting fiery darts of doubt (Ephesians 6:16), but we have to remember that the devil is already defeated and that he is the Father of Lies (Colossians 2:15; John 8:44). Every dart of doubt is a lie. The enemy hates the truth. It's at times like these that the Holy Spirit will speak words of comfort and remind you of God's promises. He will tell you things like this: "Take courage. It's not over. They will be delivered." Or He will send someone to you with a word of encouragement spoken in due season (Proverbs 15:23). A song will rise up in your spirit. Peace will come over you or a Scripture verse will come back to your memory. It is bits of encouragement like these that help keep us hopeful and renewed in our faith. We serve a very faithful, very caring, very loving, and very understanding God. He always honors His promises to us (2 Timothy 2:13; Isaiah 45:19; Isaiah 46:9–11; Isaiah 43:13).

I believe this is what God did in the allegory found in Jeremiah 31:15–17 when God said, "There is weeping in Ramah," Rachel is weeping because her children are no more and is refusing to be comforted. And the Lord, told her to weep no more because "I heard your prayers and you will see your children again. I will deliver your children from the land of their enemies and bring them back into their own borders." Then He told her, "There is hope for your future, and that her children would come again to their own border." Sometimes, we weep uncontrollably for our loved ones who might be taken over by a sin or bondage, and we long for their deliverance and restoration. What I believe is so beautiful about this Scripture passage is that God will do this for both you and I. We are told, "Call on to Me in your time of trouble, and I will answer and deliver you, and you will glorify Me." God loves to answer prayers like these because He knows the glory will go to only Him (Psalms 50:15). God loves to do the impossible (Jeremiah 32:17; Matthew 19:26), and He will do it for you too! Shall we pray?

PRAYER FOR THE HOPE OF DELIVERANCE AND REPENTANCE OF LOVED ONES

Lord, may You, comfort all those who are weeping as Rachel for their children, families, spouses, and loved ones. I (we) pray that God, the source of hope, will fill you completely with joy and peace because you trust in Him. Then you will overflow with confident hope through the power of the Holy Spirit. The Lord spoke to me again, saying: In Ramah there is bitter weeping, Rachel is weeping for her children, families, spouses, and loved ones, and she cannot be comforted, for they are gone. But the Lord says: Do not cry any longer, for I have heard your prayers and you will see them again; they will come back to you from the distant land of the enemy. There is hope for your future, says the Lord, and your children, families, spouses, and loved ones will come again to their own land. I have heard Ephraim's groans: "You have punished me greatly; but I needed it all, as a calf must be trained for the yoke. Turn me again to You and restore me, for You alone are God, but I was sorry afterwards, I kicked myself for my stupidity. I was thoroughly ashamed of all that I did in younger days." And the Lord replies: Ephraim is still my son (daughter), my darling child I had to punish him (her), but I still love him (her). I long for him (her) and surely will have mercy on him (her). In Jesus' name, amen (Jeremiah 31:15, Romans 15:13, Jeremiah 31:15-20).

CHAPTER EIGHT

DELIVERANCE FROM BESETTING SINS AND BONDAGE

God wants His people to be delivered and to be totally set free from besetting sins and bondage (Hebrews 12:1; Galatian 5:1). There are many Christians living defeated lives because of sin(s) and/or bondage. A besetting sin is any habitually occurring sin that takes place frequently. An example of this is Moses' anger with the children of Israel in the wilderness (Exodus 32:19; Numbers 20:8–12) or the children of Israel idolatry (Exodus 32:1–33:4; Judges 8:33; Jeremiah 23:27). A bondage is anything that keeps an individual from reaching his or her potential and keeps him or her in a place of stagnation (Exodus 20:13; 2 Chronicles 26:16–21; 1 Kings 11:1–13; Hosea 4:11). God desires that all of His children live victorious lives free from habitual sins, besetting sin, and bondage (Galatians 5:1). God said that we have not because we ask not (James 4:2). We need to start asking God to set us and others free from all our besetting sins and bondages. Why live underneath our privilege as the children of the light, especially when Jesus came to set us free so that we might have the abundant life (Luke 4:18; John 10:10), which encompasses every area of our lives? We are told that whom the Son set free is free indeed (John 8:36). We can have freedom in Christ to live the kind of lives He intended for each of us to live (Galatians 5:13; James 4:13-15; Titus 2:12;3:8; 2 Peter 3:11–12, 18; 1 John 1:7). We can start today by asking God to create within us a new clean heart and by renewing a rightful spirit within us (Psalms 51:10). Then we need to repent of whatever sins the Father reveals to us and start aligning ourselves to His Word and will for our lives (Joel 2:12–13; Galatians 6:2; 2 Peter 3:18; Luke 22:42).

This kind of freedom only happens when we are truthful and transparent with God. It is saying, "God, I have blown it. I'm stuck in a rut, and I need You to help me carry this load or change the course of my life now (Psalms 30:6–8; Psalms 25:11,16,17,18, Psalms 145:14; Psalms 27:11; Psalms 25:9)! I repent for not doing things Your way and for insisting on doing things my way" (Hosea 5:15; 6:1–3). And when this is done with sincerity, God will help as He promised in His Word (Psalms 145:18).

PRAYER FOR DELIVERANCE FROM BESETTING SINS

Since we are surrounded by such a great cloud of witnesses, let us lay aside every weight and the sin which does so easily beset us. Keep your servant(s) from willful sins; may they not rule over me (us). Then I (we) will be blameless, innocent of great transgression. Lord, You said, it's Your Holy Spirit at work within me (us) to do what He wants. Direct my (our) footsteps according to Your Word; let no sin rule over me (us). For the sake of Your name, O Lord, forgive my (our) iniquity, though it is great. Create in me (us) a new clean heart and renew a right spirit within me (us). Lead me (us) back into Your paths of righteousness for Your name sake. The Lord is good and glad to teach the proper path to all who go astray, and when I (we) obey Him, every path He guides us on is fragrant with His loving-kindness and His truth. Lord, my (our) sins! How many are they! Oh, pardon them for the honor of Your name. In Jesus' name, amen (Hebrews 12:1, Psalms 19:13 Philippians 2:13, Psalms 119:133, Psalms 25:11, Psalms 51:10, Psalms 25:8-11).

PRAYER FOR PEOPLE FREEDOM FROM BONDAGE

Lord, You said, that it is God's anointing that breaks every yoke. Dear Heavenly Father, please set name of person(s) free from the chains binding him/her/them. Lord, You said, that which is impossible with man (woman) is possible with You. Set them free from food addictions, eating disorders, soul ties, abusive relationships, drug addictions, alcohol addictions, nicotine, gambling, compulsive shopping and spending, love of money, obsessive-compulsive disorders, fear, anger and hostility, stealing, corporate greed, greed, pride, lust, sexual immorality, homosexual lifestyles, pornography, and any other bondage. You said that, whatever I (we) bind on earth is bound in heaven and whatever I (we) loose on earth is loosed in heaven. And I (we) loose conviction, repentance, deliverance, and (name any other things that you or they need deliverance from here). You said, whom the Son has set free is free indeed. And may he/she/they be not tangled again in the same bondage of sin. I (we) declare that these afflictions will not arise a second time, because God has put an utter end to them. In Jesus' name, amen (Isaiah 10:27; Nahum 1:13; Luke 18:27; Matthew 18:18; John 8:36; Galatians 5:1; Nahum 1:9).

CHAPTER NINE

SPEAKING TO THE TREES AND MOUNTAINS IN LIFE

God gave us incredible power to speak to our lives, to speak things into existence in our lives, and the lives of others (Romans 4:17). We have been given the power of life and death in our tongues (Proverbs 18:21). We can either speak words of life or death. It's our choice to decide, but whatever choice we decide, we will have the fruit of our lips—words. We have what we say. If you only say negative, death-filled words, you will have a life filled with death, but if you train yourself to say positive, life-filled words, you will have a life teeming with Zoe (Proverbs 13:2–3). In Mark 11, Jesus showed us this very powerful principle in action. He demonstrated to us how we can speak to things that are in disarray in our lives, and how they will come into order and will become manifested. However, we must first believe and receive and have no doubt. We can command what is planted that the Father did not plant to stop bearing fruit and never manifest again (Mark 11:13–14; Matthew 15:13). We can also command mountains to depart from our lives and for them to never return again (Matthew 17:20).

All this is simply done by just getting into agreement with what God's Word says and speaking and believing and receiving what He says (Mark 11:23–24). God is no respect of persons (Romans 2:11). This spiritual principle that Jesus shared with His disciples, will work if you apply it with faith. Everything that God gives is meant for our development so that we may become mature fruit-bearing Christians lacking nothing. So let's start putting into practice this very powerful spiritual principle. Shall we start?

PRAYER FOR SPEAKING TO THE TREES AND MOUNTAINS IN LIFE

I declare and decree according to Mark 11:14, 21–24; Psalms 103:20; Hebrews 1:7, 14; Matthews 16:19. Jesus said unto the tree, "May no one ever eat fruit from you again." And I say to this tree name the tree(s) may no one ever eat fruit from you again, and I curse you to the roots and command you to wither and die in Jesus' name. Jesus, said have faith in God, truly I tell you, if anyone says to this mountain, "Go throw yourself into the sea, and does not doubt in their heart but believes that what they say will happen, it will be done for them. Therefore, I tell you, whatever you ask for in prayer, believe that you have received it and it will be yours." I say to the mountain(s), "Go throw yourself into the sea." Father, I believe and so now I receive the corresponding response. Now you His angels, You Mighty Ones who do His bidding, who obey His Word, you servants of flames of fire, who are ministering spirits sent to serve those who would inherit salvation, start the recovery process now. Go and bring the full manifestation of this declaration and decree now. In Jesus' name, so be it. Amen.

CHAPTER TEN

HURTING PEOPLE

Have you or has anyone you know been hurt? Then chances are you need deliverance. It is noted that hurt people hurt others. Without deliverance, the cycle of abuse will continue. In 1 Chronicles 4:9–10, there's a brief description of a man by the name of Jabez. Jabez was more distinguished than any of his brothers, but this was not always the case. Jabez's name means "To cause pain" because his mother had a difficult time giving birth to him. In biblical times names often had meanings unlike those in our contemporary times. Your name in biblical times was a prophetic sign of what you would become later in life. Jabez must have felt discomfort, knowing he had caused his mother pain during birth. So Jabez prayed to the God of Israel and said, "Oh, that You would bless me indeed and enlarge my territory, that Your hand would be with me and that You would keep me from evil, that I may not cause pain!" And God granted him what he requested. If you look at verse 10, you'll see that Jabez asked God to help keep him from evil so that he may not cause pain. You will notice in this passage of Scripture that Jabez took the initiative for his own deliverance and God granted him his heart's desire, which was to be effective and productive and to break the cycle of pain so that he would not hurt others. You and I at times must do likewise, or else we will go through life hurting others and being hurt in return. Notice that Jabez asked God first and that God responded by delivering him. Other examples, of hurting people in the Word of God include Joseph, Benjamin, Joseph's little brother, Ruth and Naomi.

What do Jabez, Joseph, Benjamin, Ruth and Naomi have in common? The answer, they all experienced or caused pain, and God reversed, delivered, healed, and distinguished them all. Joseph was sold into slavery in Egypt by his ten older brothers, who were all jealous of him because he was his father's favorite son, born to Jacob in his old age by his favorite wife, Rachael. He also gave him a coat of many colors (Genesis 37:3–29). A short time later he was bought by a member of the personal staff of Pharaoh, who was the king of Egypt (Genesis 37:36). While Joseph was in Potiphar house, God was with him and blessed and prospered him in everything he did (Genesis 39:2–6). Sometime after this his master's, Potiphar's, wife tried to seduce him, but he evaded her advances. He was falsely accused of rape and was thrown in prison (Genesis 39:7–20). However, Joseph did not become bitter, hateful, angry, or revengeful, so God blessed and favored him and everything that he did. Joseph prospered in everything he did because God was with him (Genesis 39:21–23). In both Potiphar's house and prison Joseph prospered because God was with him and favored him. Two years later Joseph was taken from the prison, where he served as the administrator, and was brought to the Palace (Genesis 41:14). Pharaoh had a dream that no one could interpret but Joseph (Genesis 41:1–13, 15–36). As a result, he was promoted to the second in charge of Egypt (Genesis 41:37–44), and God vindicated Joseph when his 10 older brothers who sold him into slavery in Egypt, came to Egypt bowing before him when they were buying food during the famine in the land of Canaan (Genesis 41:56-57, Genesis 42:1-6).

Genesis 35:17 gives a brief description of the birth of Benjamin, Joseph's younger brother who was originally named Ben-oni by his mother, Rachel, Ben-oni, which means the "Son of my sorrow." Rachel named her son this because she was dying while birthing him. But, in Genesis 35:18, Jacob objected and renamed the child Benjamin, meaning "Son of my right hand." Essentially, you can see how God changed Benjamin's destiny from that of pain and loss to that of favor and success (Genesis 42:38; 43:29, 34; 45:21–22).

Lastly there is Naomi and Ruth. Now, Naomi's husband, Elimelech, and their two sons were originally from Israel, but they relocated to Moab because of a famine. During the course of her stay her sons, Mahlon and Chilion, married both Moabites, women named Orpah and Ruth. Naomi lost her husband and was left with her two married sons. Later Mahlon and Chilion died. Ruth, Orpah, and Naomi all experienced the pain of bereavement of their husbands while living in Moab. Orpah lost her husband, Chilion, and Ruth lost her husband, Mahlon. Naomi lost both her husband, Elimelech, and her two sons (Ruth 1:3–5). Now, Naomi, daughter in-law Orpah returned back to her people, but Ruth stayed and followed her mother-in-law, Naomi. They went back to Israel because of another famine in Moab and the report that God had blessed Israel with abundance of crops (Ruth 1:7–22). God restored both Ruth and Naomi lives by repaying them with two mercies for each of their troubles (Ruth 2:1–23). Ruth remarried a man named Boaz, who was Naomi's close relative and who later became Ruth's husband redeemer, and Naomi was able to raise her grandchild (Ruth 3; 4).

Lastly, God is in the healing and restoring business. He wants to heal and restore you and your loved ones to a greater state of well-being

(Psalms 147:3; Joel 2:25; Haggai 2:9). He wants to restore your hopes and dreams and give you a new beginning (Jeremiah 29:5–7, 11; Isaiah 43:18–19). This is the heart of the Father, but you have to ask first. Shall we go to the Throne of Grace?

PRAYER OF DELIVERANCE
FOR HURTING PEOPLE

Lord, heal name(s) of person(s)', including yourself if you need healing, broken heart(s) and bind my/his/her/their/our wounds. Return back to the Lord you prisoner of hope, for I will even give you two mercies for every woe. Surround me/him/her/them/us with favor like a shield. Lord, make me/him/her/them/us glad in proportion to my/his/her/their/our former misery and replace the evil years with good. Though You have made me/him/her/them/us see troubles, many and bitter. You will restore my/his/her/their/our life (lives) again from the depths of the earth. You will increase my/his/her/their/our honor and comfort me/him/her/them/us once again. Oh, that You, would bless me/him/her/them/us and enlarge my/his/her/their/our territory, let Your hand be with me/him/her/them/us and keep me/him/her/them/us from harm so that I/he/she/they/we will be free from pain. Taste and see that the Lord is good and Your love endures forever. Lord, You said, "I will do a new thing in my/his/her/their/our life (lives), and it will spring forth today." And may these dry bones live again to spring forth to the newness of life. In Jesus' name, amen (Psalms 147:3, Zechariah 9:12; Psalms 5:12, Psalms 90:15; Psalms 71:20-21, 1 Chronicles 4:10, Psalms 34:8, Psalms 136; Isaiah 43:19; Ezekiel 37:4–5).

CHAPTER ELEVEN

PROTECTION FOR OUR CHILDREN

Children are a reward from the Lord, and they need to be greatly protected. Our adversary, the devil, knows these children will grow up and become fruit-bearing adults, so he plans attacks on them before they reach maturity. So as a result, our children are under attack comparable to that of times of Moses and Jesus (Exodus 1:12–22; Matthew 2:1–18). That's why our prayers are needed to circumvent the plans of the devil against our children and to loose God's plans over them (John 17:9–15). We are told in the Word of God that He has a plan for us that's for good and not evil, but to give us a future and hope (Jeremiah 29:11). I believe this plan includes our children and future generations to come (Jeremiah 29:5–7). When we pray, speak God's Word, and speak blessings over them, they come under the shelter of God's wings (Psalms 91:1; Jeremiah 31:15–17; Deuteronomy 6:2, 20–25). We are told that no good thing will God withhold from us, and this includes the protection of our children (Psalms 84:11; Psalms 115:14). Our children will live and not die but will declare the works of the Lord and will live to be a ripe old age and will not be harvested before their time (Psalms 118:17; Psalms 91:16; Job 5:25). God does and will answer our prayers for our children since He was the one who gave them to us in the first place (Matthew 7:10–11). God gave us many promises about protecting us, and I believe this includes our children. We are told that that if anyone hurts one of these little children, their angels will report it, and the person(s) be punished (Matthew 18:10–11). Another way to ensure our children stay protected is by living holy and having reverence for God because it guarantees many blessings that will come upon our children and future generations (Deuteronomy 4:9–10,40;Psalms 112:1–2; Psalms 128; Proverbs 14:26; Psalms 25:12-13). This is because living upright before God protects our posterity. Is God awesome or what?

PRAYER FOR THE PROTECTION
OF OUR CHILDREN

Heavenly Father, we boldly approach Your Throne of Grace to obtain help in the time of trouble. You said to call upon You in the time of trouble and You would answer and deliver us and You would get the glory. You said to be anxious for nothing but everything by prayer and supplication with thanksgiving, let our requests be made known to You; and the peace of God, which surpasses all understanding, will guard our hearts and minds through Christ Jesus. Lord, we know that You are able to do exceedingly abundantly above that which we could ever ask, hope, think, wish, dream, or pray because power belongs to You and nothing is too difficult for You. So we are petitioning You today on the behalf of our children. We know there is an all-out assault against our children. We plead the Blood of Jesus over every boy and girl and youth. We ask that You place a hedge of protection around them and keep them from all harm. Lord, there are people targeting our children at the malls, particularly little girls, with the hopes of using them for sex-trafficking. Lord, reveal these practices and expose these individuals. Give our children an uncanny awareness for potential harm and a supernatural discernment of strangers and their intentions. Let them feel unusual discomfort around those with impure intentions. Lord, You said in Your Word that there is nothing hidden that will not be revealed and nothing in darkness that will not be brought to light. Lord, we ask that You would please help some girl, some boy, some youth who have been kidnapped to escape their captors this day. We plead the Blood of Jesus over these precious little ones with the Angel of the Lord encamped around them and the Angel of God's presence pursuing these perpetrators. We even ask that You send Angels disguised as humans to report and to lead the appropriate authorities to where these illegal activities are taking place right now. We also ask that You help and enable husbands and single fathers to take full responsibility for their children regardless of their jobs, personal responsibilities, and current relationship status with the mother of their children. Help mothers to stop using their children as weapons to punish their fathers by not allowing these men to be present or participate in their children's lives. Open these women's eyes so that they can see the damage that can occur when they deny fathers an active roles in their children's lives. Let them see that this actually hurts their children's social development. Help these women to mature and realize that every child needs both a mother and father, regardless if they are together or not. In Jesus' name, we pray. Amen (Hebrews 4:16; Psalms 50:14–15; Philippians 4:6–7; Ephesians 3:20; Psalms 62:11; 68:34, Jeremiah 32:17, 27; Ephesians 6:18; Job 1:10; Psalms 34:7, 20; 31:20-21; 33:20,Mark 4:22; Matthew 12:34; John 7:1, 19; 8:59; Acts 16:6–7; Luke 22:21, 47–48; Luke 22:21; John 13:21; Luke 8:17; Acts 12:5-12; Psalms 34:7; Psalms 35:6; Genesis 37:15–17; Genesis 19:1-3; Hebrews 13:2; 1 Timothy 5:8; Proverbs 22:6; Ephesians 6:4; Proverbs 14:1-2; Titus 2:4–5, 12).

CHAPTER TWELVE

MARRIAGE OVERVIEW

God wants the institution of marriage to be taken very seriously and to be held in very high esteem. "Why?" you may ask. Well, here are a few reasons: This institution can combat loneliness, encourage people to procreate, and demonstrate what the kingdom of God is like (Genesis 2:18; 1:28; Ephesians 5:23–32). When God created man— that is Adam in the Garden of Eden—God saw that Adam was alone. Then God said, "It is not good for man to be alone, so I will make him a helpmate who is suitable for him (Genesis 2:18–22)." Guess who that helpmate was? You guessed it—Eve (Genesis 2:23-24). Did you know that before God created the church, He created the institution of marriage and then the family unit (Genesis 2:18–24; 3:20; 4:1)? Marriage and family are God's design because He wants godly offspring (Malachi 2:15). God wants the earth populated with godly people, and marriage is the best way to accomplish this goal (Genesis 6:4–22– 7:1, 5–9:1, 7; Malachi 2:15). Marriage was designed by God to demonstrate what the Kingdom of God looks like. The husband is meant to be the direct representation of Christ to his bride, and the wife is meant to reflect the role of the church (Ephesians 5:23–27, 32). The husband's love for his bride is also meant to reflect Christ's love for the church (Ephesians 5:25). Christ loved the church. Christ nurtured the church, cherished the church, and He gave Himself unselfishly for the church (Ephesians 5:29). This is how husbands are to love their wives. But because we live in a sinful fallen world, people often deviate from God's plan.

You see, countless men and women standing before God in front of a church full of witnesses or before a justice of peace and totally transgress their marriage vows they made to each other a year or several years later, due to not counting the cost of (Proverbs 20:25), not taking their vows seriously or due to perjury (Proverbs 12:22; Ecclesiastes 5:4; Deuteronomy 23:21, 23; Psalms 50:14; Malachi 3:5, Deuteronomy 5:11) abuse, marital infidelity, selfishness, and the list goes on. Lust, adultery, and divorce all break God's heart, and all are consider evil (Malachi 2:13-16; Mark 7:21; Proverbs 21:4). It should be noted, that divorce is only permissible when adultery occurs or when an unbelieving spouse leaves (Matthew 5:32; 1 Corinthians 7:10-11). Marriage is a very beautiful gift when people enter into it soberly, take it seriously, and have the right perspective. But when the institution of marriage is taken lightly, perspectives are wrong, and priorities are not in order, it can lead to brokenness and even divorce. Even if your marriage suffers a setback or is broken, that does not mean it needs to end. Broken marriages can be restored and God can make all things new. The God we serve is a repairer of the breach (Ezekiel 13:5), a God of restoration (Joel 2:25), and a God of new beginnings (Isaiah 43:18-19). He is famous for making all things new (2 Corinthians 5:17; Ezekiel 36:26; Ephesians 4:24). He specializes in turnarounds and recoveries (1 Samuel 30:18-20) and quickens dead things (Romans 4:17). We need to pray for all aspects of our marriages and those we are called to intercede for. We can pray to help husbands and wives to take better responsibility for their marriages, to avoid the temptation to commit adultery, or to be delivered from adultery. We live in a sex-crazed culture where everywhere you look the glamorization of adultery is very pervasive in our culture from television programs, music, friends, acquaintances, and the list goes on. It is not the temptation that is sin, but it is acting on the impulse to cheat that is.

There is temptation everywhere, and many have caved under the pressure. In Luke 17:1, we are told that temptation to sin will come but woe to the one who does the tempting. There are consequences for adultery, such as dishonor and marred reputation, loss of wealth and broken dreams, venereal diseases, children from adultery, divorce, broken homes, disappointed relatives and friends, guilty consciences, God's wrath, and eternal damnation if it is not repented of (Proverbs 5:9-17, 21, 22;6:29, 32; 2 Samuel 11; 2 Samuel 12:1–18; Proverbs 2:16-22; 7:24-27; Revelation 21:27; 22:15).

PRAYER FOR MARITAL RESPONSIBILITY

Lord, let no husband or wife take lightly the institution of marriage. May we (they) be given the understanding of what You require of us (them) as husband and wife. May we (they) be willing to follow Your guidance, knowing that You would not give us (them) a task that we (they) could not handle. Give husbands the desire and the ability to lead as You prompt. May husbands not be controlled by pride, anger, fear, selfishness, or self-seeking behavior, but may they be led by Your Holy Spirit because You said, that many who are led by the Spirit are the sons of God. May they see every situation as You see it. May neither husbands nor wives exalt their own thoughts above Your Word but bring every thought into captivity through the obedience of Christ Jesus. Help us (them) to guard (our) their spirits, souls, hearts, minds, thoughts, and decisions from all deception. May all lies masquerading as truth be exposed and brought into the light. May we (they) walk in the light as You are in the light. May the Spirit of Truth guide (us) them into all truth because You said, "You shall know the truth and the truth shall set you free." Enable us (them) to walk and live in obedience to Your laws, promptings, and leadings. Forgive us (them) for times of failure and for causing Your Holy Spirit grief. You said, that it is the Holy Spirit that lives inside of us (them), causing us (them) to will and do Your perfect pleasure. Release us (them) to become the husbands and wives you have ordained us (them) to be. In Jesus' name, amen (Hebrews 13:4; 1 Thessalonians 4:6; 1 Corinthians 6:9, 1 Corinthians 10:13; Romans 13:14; Romans 12:3, Colossians 3:19; Ephesians 4:31; 2 Timothy 1:7; Romans 8:15; Revelation 21:8; Philippians 2:3–4; 4:5;

Romans 8:14; Revelation 21:8; Philippians 2:3-4, 4:5; 2 Corinthians 10:4, Proverbs 5:23; Ephesians 5:6; Proverbs 12:12; 1 John 1:7; John8:32; Psalms 119:11, Psalms 37:31; Proverbs 3:5; Psalms 23:3, Psalms 51:10; Ephesians 4:30; Philippians 2:13; Ephesians 5:21).

PRAYER AGAINST THE TEMPTATION TO COMMIT ADULTERY

Lord, You, said marriage is an honorable institution among all and the marriage bed is undefiled, but fornicators and adulterers God will judge. Lord, You, also said here's another thing you do. You cover the Lord's altar with tears, weeping, and groaning because He pays no attention to your offerings and does not accept them with pleasure. You cry out, "Why does not the Lord except my worship?" I tell you why! Because the Lord witnessed the vows you and your wife made when you were young. But you have been unfaithful to her, though she remained your faithful partner, the wife of your marriage vows. Did not the Lord make you one with your wife? In body and spirit you are His. And what does He want? Godly children from your union, so guard your heart; remain loyal to the wife of your youth. "For I hate divorce!" Says the Lord, the God of Israel. "To divorce your wife is to overwhelm her with cruelty," says the Lord of Heavens Armies. "So guard your heart; do not be unfaithful to your wife." Do not lust after strange women beauty. Do not let her coy glances seduce you. For a prostitute will bring you to poverty, but sleeping with another man's wife will cost you your life. A man who looks at a woman with lust in his heart has already committed adultery with her in his heart. The man who commits adultery is an utter fool, for he destroys himself. He will be wounded and disgraced. This shame will never be erased. Can a man scoop a flame into his lap and not have his clothes catch on fire? Can he walk on hot coals and not blister his feet? So it is with the man who sleeps with another man's wife. He who embraces her will not go unpunished. My son, pay attention to my wisdom; listen carefully to my wise counsel. For the lips of an immoral woman are as sweet as honey, and her mouth is smoother than oil. But in the end she is as bitter as poison, as dangerous as a double – edged sword. Her feet go down to death; her steps lead straight to hell. For she does not know the path to life. She staggers down a crooked trail and does not even realize where it leads. Stay away from her! Do not go near the door of her house! If you do, you will lose your honor and will lose to merciless people all you have achieved. Strangers will consume your wealth and someone else will enjoy the fruits of your labor. In the end, you will groan in anguish when disease consumes your body. You will say, "how I hated discipline! If only I had not ignored all the warnings! I have come to the brink of utter ruin, and now I must face public disgrace." Drink water from your own well—share your love only with your wife. Why spill the water of your springs in the streets, having sex with just anyone? Be faithful and true to your wife. Why should you beget children with women of the street? Why share your children with those outside your home? You should reserve it for yourselves. Never share it with strangers. Let your manhood be a blessing. Let your wife be a fountain of blessing for you. Rejoice in the wife of your youth. She is a loving deer, a graceful doe. Let her breast satisfy you always. May you always be captivated by her love. Why be captivated my son, by an immoral woman or fondle the breast of a promiscuous woman? Why delight yourself with promiscuous women, embracing what is not yours? For the Lord sees clearly what a man does, examining every path he takes. There is a way that seems right, but the end result is death. Spirit of Truth lead name of person(s) into all truth and understanding and may (name of person(s) not be wise in his/her/their eyes, but rather may he/she/they depart from evil. Give revelatory wisdom and knowledge right now that adultery is a great offense in Heaven's Court. Lift the veil from his/her/their eyes to see the truth. Give them an uncanny awareness that You are always watching and are recording everything he/she/they are doing and thinking and that they will have to give an account of everything they have done or thought. Let there be a reverential fear of God formed in their minds and personalities. May their greatest desire be to please You and have You say, "Well done, My good and faithful servant. You may now enter into My Rest." In Jesus' name, amen (Hebrews 13:4; Malachi 2:13–16; Proverbs 6:25–26; Matthew 5:28; Proverbs 6:32-33, 6:27-29,5:1, 5:3-6, 5:8-21, Proverbs 14:12, John 16:13; Proverbs 3:7, Acts 9:18; Hebrews 4:13, Jeremiah 16:17; Jeremiah 32:19; Psalms 86:11; Matthew 25:23).

PRAYER FOR REPENTANCE OF ADULTERY

For the wisdom of this world is foolishness in God's sight. As it is written: He catches the wise in their craftiness. For the Lord sees clearly what a person does, examining every path he (she) takes. An evil man (woman) is held captive by his (her) own lust. They are ropes that catch and hold him (her), and again the Lord knows that the thoughts of the wise are futile. You can be sure that your sins will find you out. There is a way that seems right to a man (woman), but the end result is death; be not wise in your own eyes, but rather fear God and depart from evil. Do not be deceived God is not mocked, for whatsoever a man (woman) sowth, that's what he (she) will also receive. If he (she) sows to the flesh, there comes death and destruction, but if he (she) sows to the Spirit, he (she) will have life in peace. Adultery is a great offense in Heaven's Court. The wages of sin is death. Repent and turn from your sins so that times of refreshing may come from the Lord. Repent and turn from your sins so that your sins can be blotted out. Lord, make the crooked places straight. A man (woman) who turns from the path of righteousness, even his (her) prayers are an abomination. May they realized there is nothing hidden that will not be made known and there is nothing in darkness that will not be brought to light. He (she) that covers up his (her) sins will not prosper, but he (she) that confesses their sins and do away with them will be given a second chance. May he (she) be given the revelation that they will someday have to give an account to You, the One whom there is no shadow of turning and the One who sees everything, even that which is hidden because a man's (woman's) ways are in God's full view. May spouse or person(s) name say as David,

"When I kept silent, my bones wasted away through my groaning all day long. For day and night Your hand was heavy on me; my strength was sapped as the heat of the summer. Then I acknowledged my sin to You and did not cover up my iniquity. I said, 'I will confess my transgressions to the Lord.' And, You forgave the guilt of my sins." Many sorrows will come to the wicked, but the Lord's unfailing love surrounds the ones who trust in Him. It's a terrible thing to fall into the hands of the living God. He is a God of Justice. You can be assured of this; your sins will find you out. You also, can be assured that pride will not go unpunished and that He will make the crooked places straight. When God punishes a man (woman); he (she) does not return to the same sin. With God there is a time and then judgment and everyone who belongs to God He corrects. Notice how God is both kind and severe towards those who disobey but kind to you if you continue to trust in His kindness. But if you stop trusting, you also will be cut off. For God did not spare the natural branches, He will not spare you. As a calf must be trained for the yoke. Turn him/her/them again to You and restore. May he/she/they say, that You are God alone and that I was sorry afterwards. I kicked myself for my stupidity. I was thoroughly ashamed of all I did in younger days and the Lord replies, "Ephraim is still my son (daughter), my darling child. I had to punish him (her), but I still love him (her). I long for him (her) and surely will have mercy on him (her)." In Jesus' name, amen. (1 Corinthians 3:19; Proverbs 5:21–22, 1 Corinthians 3:20, Numbers 32:23; Proverbs 14:12, Proverbs 3:7, Galatians 6:7–8; Romans 6:23; Acts 3:19; Isaiah 45:2, Proverbs 28:9, Luke 8:17; 2 Corinthians 5:10, 1 Peter 4:5; Proverbs 28:13, Hebrews 4:13; Psalms 32:3–5, 10; Hebrews 10:31, Isaiah 61:8, Numbers 32:23, Proverbs 16:5, Isaiah 45:2, Psalms 119:67,71; Jeremiah 31:18–19; Hebrews 12:11, Ecclesiastes 12:14, Hebrews 12:6, Romans 11:22-23, Jeremiah 31:18-20).

CHAPTER THIRTEEN

DELIVERANCE FROM ABUSE IN MARRIAGE

Abuse is rampant in the world we live in today and it is affecting every facet of our society, and it has even trickled down into the church. There are many women and children suffering from spousal abuse within the four walls of the church. This is not a popular subject but there must be an open dialogue. Countless women and children are suffering at the hands of their husbands and fathers. And what I found was that many of these women are very intelligent, very well educated, very successful, very prominent and are from very prominent families. This demystifies the perception that spousal abuse is only happening to women who are in poverty, who are uneducated, and who come from broken homes. Spousal abuse is epidemic in our modern society and affects both the rich and poor alike. Spousal abuse does not discriminate. It is a topic that very few want to discuss, and churches are often dismissive and ill-equipped to address the issue of spousal abuse among their members. Countless women have gone to their clergy and pastoral care departments, looking for assistance there, and they are often left feeling judged, abandoned, and isolated. They are also, made to feel that it's their fault and that they somehow provoked their husbands. Some even are given the advice to, "Submit to your husbands as unto the Lord and to do whatever he tells you to do." Many women are left feeling dejected, unheard, and uncared for. They feel that their issues are not pertinent to the church.

In 2 Timothy 3:2, we are told that in the end times people would be abusive, and this is very evident in our culture today. This behavior is present in many marriages, including those in the body of Christ today. However, we know we have an Advocate in Heaven who will answer us when we pray (Hebrews 4:15). We are exhorted in Ephesians 6:18 to pray in the Spirit on all occasions and make supplications for the saints everywhere. We are also exhorted in 1 John 5:16 if you see a Christian brother or sister sinning in a way that does not lead to death, you should pray, and God will give that person life. If you know someone being abused, do not keep quiet (Proverbs 3:27; Galatians 6:10). Please, stand in the gap for them through prayer and help them escape the abuse (1 Samuel 12:23; Proverbs 31:8–9; Isaiah 1:17; Proverbs 29:7; Jeremiah 22:16). There are resources available for abused women and children, such as the Domestic Violence Hotline (1.800.787.3224). You can go to your local court and police station to file a restraining order, and there are support groups for battered women, too. God never intended for any of His precious daughters to be abused in marriage under the guise of submission (Malachi 2:13–15; 1 Peter 3:7). Yes, wives are to submit to their husbands and to show them respect but only in love and not out of fear (Ephesians 5:24, 33).

God is a God of order and love (1 Corinthians 14:33; Isaiah 61:8). And abuse is disorderly and not very loving. Abuse is a gross misrepresentation of Christ because the husband is an utter representation of Jesus and the wife is a representation of the church, and Jesus is not an abuser

(Ephesian 5:22–33). Jesus gave His life for the church and loved and nurtured the church. He did not abused the church (Ephesians 5:25, 28, 29). Abusive husbands most often blame their wives for the abuse and often refuse to take responsibility for their abusive behavior. I believe this is because most abusers have a distorted image of themselves and they tend to see themselves as the epitome of perfection and incapable of imperfection (Proverbs 30:12; 16:2; Titus 1:16; Luke 18:11). So when abuse occurs, they project the reason(s) for the abuse unto their wives and will often make many *you* and *if* statements. "You made me angry." "If you would've did it my way, then I wouldn't have hurt you." I believe these *if* and *you* statements stem from a sense of entitlement that these husbands often have, which often contributes to their developing a feeling of superiority over their wives – that is I am better than you, so I can do what I want and trample your rights. Blame is often used to escape responsibility for their abuse. Abusive husbands were often abused as children and mostly grew up in homes or families where abuse was commonplace. There are many abusive husbands in the Body of Christ who hate their behavior and want desperately to be delivered (Romans 7:15–25). God is a deliverer and restorer, and I believe God wants to deliver and heal both the abuser and the abused (Psalms 18:2; Exodus 15:2; Job 5:18–19). This prayer serves to minister deliverance for both the abused and the abuser. Let us pray and watch God bring the strongholds of spousal abuse down and release healing, breakthrough, restoration, and recovery (2 Corinthians 10:4–5; Psalms 107:19–20; 6:2; Micah 2:13; 2 Samuel 5:20; Joel 2:25; 1 Samuel 30:8,18). God will make all things new.

PRAYER FOR DELIVERANCE OF
ABUSE IN MARRIAGE

Lord, You said I (we) can boldly approach Your Throne of Grace to obtain help in the time of trouble and that I (we) can call on You in the time of trouble and You would answer and deliver us and You would receive the glory. Well, Father God, I (we) ask that You expose and end the sin of spousal abuse among Christian husbands against their wives and children, whether it be in church leaders or church members. I (we) pray that You will bring a spirit of conviction, repentance, and deliverance. Please, heal the wives and children (<u>you can include yourself and children, too</u>) at the receiving end of the abuse. I (we) bind the spirit of shame and condemnation in wives and their children (<u>you can include yourself and children, too</u>). I (we) loose the revelation that I am/we/they are not responsible for my/our/their husband(s) and my/our/their father(s) abuse. I/we/they do not have to wear the shame nor is there any condemnation in me/us/them. I (we) loose the complete restoration, recovery, and any healing of any wounds both physically and emotionally and broken hearts resulting from abuse. I (we) loose the freedom for me/us/them to become all God intended for me/us/them to become. I (we) loose the Hounds of Heaven to convict these husbands and fathers right now and to bring the necessary correction and discipline for these men. I (we) loose the Lord opening their eyes right now, because faith is right now, so that they can see how abusive they really are and the direct result of their actions. I (we) loose godly remorse in these men that leads to repentance right now. I (we) loose these men apologizing, developing the fruit of the Spirit, developing godly behavior under the guidance of the Holy Spirit toward me/us/them as his (their) wife (wives) and children as ascribed in the Bible: Husbands, do not deal treacherously with the wives of your youth; husbands, do not be harsh, resentful, or be critical of your wives; husbands, love your wives as Christ loves the church and give yourselves for them. So ought men to love their wives as their own bodies; he who loves his wife loves himself. After all, no one ever hated their own bodies, but they nourish and cherishes it; husbands, live with your wives in honor as the weaker vessel in treating her as you should so that your prayers are not hindered. Fathers, do not provoke your children to wrath. I (we) bind husbands using control, threats, domineering behavior, manipulation, anger, withholding love and affection, withholding encouragement, withholding wealth and financial resources from our (their) family (families), and refusing to account where the income is being spent. In Jesus' name, I (we) bind all generational curses and negative attributes passed down from one generation to another generation in these men's lives in the name of Jesus. And, I (we) bind all of these maladaptive ways of acting and responding towards us (them) as their wives and children through the Blood of Jesus. And, I (we) loose an inner healing and release from old ways of behaving and responding, and I (we) cancel this old program through the Blood of Jesus. I (we) loose that the old things have passed away; behold, all things have become new in these men. And, I (we) call forth the regenerative nature of Christ to be activated right now in their souls, hearts, minds, thinking, purposes and are now being displayed in their actions, choices, decisions, and leadership of our (their) family (families) and homes; also, are now being exhibited right now in their display of love towards us as their wives and our children in the name of Jesus and through the Blood of Jesus. I (we) loose in the name of Jesus that these men are no longer abusive, angry, controlling, manipulative, domineering, selfish, self-seeking, and/or withholding of love and affection, wealth or financial resources. I (we) decree and declare: that these afflictions will not arise a second time because God has put an utter end to it in Jesus' name. I (we) loose instead, these men are loving and kind, thoughtful and considerate, spirit-filled, spirit-controlled, spirit-led, thinking of the greater good of their wives and children. Also, they are generous, self-sacrificing, and helpful toward us as their wives and children. I (we) declare that when conflict arises, they seek the Lord's Counsel and they are obedient to His leading. They do nothing out of selfish-ambitious and are not concerned about only their affairs but the affairs of their wives and children in the name of Jesus and through the Blood of Jesus. I (we) decree, declare, and loose that we as their wives are contented in our homes, whether we have careers or are homemakers, as long as our husbands are submitted to the Lordship of Christ and loving (us) their wives as Christ loves the church. Their reward is prosperity and happiness; everything they do prospers in Jesus name and through the Blood of Jesus, amen. (Hebrews 4:16; Psalms 50:15; Isaiah 57:12; Luke 8:17; Matthew 18:18, Psalms 147:3, Psalms 146:8a, 2 Corinthians 7:10; Acts 16:37; Galatians 5:22; Romans 8:14; Malachi 2:15; Colossians 3:19; Ephesians 5:25,28,29; 1 Peter 3; Ephesians 6:4; Matthew 10:26; Mark 4:22; Luke 8:17, John 8:32; Malachi 2:16-17, 3:14-15, Matthew 20:25-26, Jonah 1:2–3; Titus 1:10a, 15b, 16; Romans 1:25, Proverbs 3:27–28; 1 Timothy 5:8; 1 Corinthians 7:33, 1 Corinthians 7:3-; Titus 1:16, 1 Corinthians 6:10, Exodus 34:6–7; Genesis 20:1–6; Genesis 26:7–11; John 8:32; Galatians 5:1, Galatians 3:13, 1 Corinthians 6:11, Romans 7:5, 8, Titus 3:3, Romans 7:15-25, Titus 3:4-6, 2 Corinthians 5:17, Isaiah 43:18-19, Ezekiel 36:26; Romans 12:2, 2 Corinthians 4:16, Ephesians 4:23-24, Colossians 3:10, Titus 3:5, Romans 13:14, Romans 12:1, Galatians 5:1, 1 Peter 1:15, 1 Peter 2:12, Ephesians 2:3, Ephesians

4:31, Ephesians 4:20-22, Ephesians 4:32, Ephesians 5:8-13, Nahum 1:9; Philippians 2:3–5, Ephesians 4:32, Ephesians 5:29-30, Psalms 22:4-5, Philippians 2:4, Psalms 128:3, 1 Corinthians 11:3, 1 Peter 3:7, Ephesians 5:25, Psalms 128:1-2).

CHAPTER FOURTEEN

THE BATTLE BELONGS TO THE LORD

Do you know the battle that you are currently in belongs to the Lord? Do you know it was won more than two thousand years ago on Calvary? It ended when Jesus said, "it is finished!" All we have to do is believe God's Word, get into agreement with it, and speak it over our situation. In this case, we can pray it and watch and thank God for the breakthrough (Mark 9:23; Proverbs 18:12; Romans 4:17; Psalms 50:15; Philippians 4:13). We are told in Psalms 24:8–10 that the Lord is the King of Glory. The Lord, strong and mighty, invincible in battle. Who is this King of Glory? The Commander of all of Heaven's Armies. The King of Glory is the one who fights on our behalf. When we approach His throne for help and when we place our faith in Him, we are never made ashamed for trusting Him (Psalms 25:3). Have you noticed at the start of every battle the enemy tries to taunts you with thoughts of defeat, uncertainty, doubts, and anxieties? Then to compound matters, people often try to persuade you to quit or tell you how your situation is hopeless or unchangeable due to their finite thinking. But

God made us more than conquerors. We are triumphant! "Why?" you may ask. Because we serve a very awesome God who loves to make the impossible possible, but it's only possible if we invite Him into our dilemmas. When trouble comes, God should be the first place we should go (Nahum 1:7). He is always waiting to intervene on our behalf when we go to Him in prayer. This is what both King Jehoshaphat and King Hezekiah, did when they were faced with hopeless and paralyzing circumstances from opposing enemy forces (2 Chronicles 20:1–2; Isaiah 36:1–2,12–19). They sought the Commander of Heaven's Armies (2 Chronicle 20:3–17; Isaiah 37:1–6), and He went to task on both opposing enemy forces and totally obliterated them.

The most awe-inspiring thing was that neither Jehoshaphat nor Hezekiah's army forces had to lift a finger. King Jehoshaphat fell prostrate on the ground and began worshipping God, then all the people of both Judah and Jerusalem followed suit. Then afterwards, the Levites of both Kohath and Korah clans began to praise the Lord God of Israel with songs of praise that were strong and clear (2 Chronicles 20:18–19). Then the following day the leaders determined that the choir should march out in front of the army, wearing sanctified clothes and singing this song "His Loving–Kindness Is Forever," so they walked praising and thanking God (2 Chronicles 20:21). As the choir began singing and praising, God immediately caused the united army forces arrayed against King Jehoshaphat to start fighting and destroying themselves (2 Chronicles 20:24).

In King Hezekiah's case the only course of action needed was his prayer petition to God. God replied through the Prophet Isaiah, that neither the Assyrian King nor his army would step foot in Jerusalem (Isaiah 37:33). So, that night an Angel of the Lord went to the Assyrians camp and struck 185,000 Assyrian soldiers dead (Isaiah 37:36). The King of Assyria returned to his country, where he was later murdered by one of his sons in the temple of Nisroch (Isaiah 37:37–38). King David, the warrior king, also had a similar experience as recorded in Psalms 22:6–8. He recounted a time when he was seeking and trusting God for deliverance, and he was mocked and ridiculed for trusting God. David was helped because in verse 25 he publically thanked and praised God for His awesome intervention and fulfilled the vow he made to God in front of those who revered God. As God did for these three Kings, so will God do for you and I when we seek Him for help from our enemies. Shall we pray?

THE BATTLE BELONGS TO THE LORD PRAYER

Lord, You said that I (we) can boldly approach the Throne of Grace to obtain help in the time of trouble and that I (we) can call upon You in the day of trouble, and You will deliver me (us), and I (we) will honor You. Well, Lord, I (we) call upon You this day because You said that which is impossible with man is possible with God and because You are my (our) mighty deliverer! Save your servant(s) and maidservant(s) with Your Mighty stretched out right powerful arm! Lord, I (we) come into the shelter of the Most High to find rest in the shadow of the Almighty. Lord, You alone are my (our) refuge and place of safety. In You I (we) place my (our) trust. Lord, You heard the boast and threats charged against me (us) from those who do not believe in You or have left You: that prayer, fasting, and no amount of intercession (or whatever you can think of that was spoken against your situation) would not help. Lord, Your Word says, "God has spoken once; twice I have heard this: that power belongs to God, and what You do is from eternity to eternity. No one can oppose You because You are God. Lord, You said that the king moreover, must not acquire great numbers of horses for himself or make the people returned to Egypt to get more of them, but the Lord has told you, "You are not to go back that way again." When you go to war against your enemies and you see horses and chariots and an army greater than yours, do not be afraid of them because the Lord, your God, who brought you up out of Egypt, will be with you. For the Lord, your God, is going with you! He will fight for you against your enemies, and He will give you victory. Lord, Your Word says that Your people were helped in their fighting and God handed the Hagrites and all their allies over to them because they cried out to You during their battle. So Lord, I (we) cry out to You in the mist of my (our) battle. Lord, Your word said, You will answer my (our) prayer(s) because I (we) trust in You. So Lord, I (we) cry out to You because I (we) trust in You. "With him/her/them is the arm of flesh, but with me (us) is the Lord my (our) God to help me (us) fight my (our) battles." And as the people gained confidence from what Hezekiah, the king of Judah, said, Lord, my (our) confidence is in You because there is no failure in You. You are not a respect of persons. What You did for King Hezekiah, You most certainly will do for me (us)! Lord, Your Word says, that a horse is a vain hope for deliverance; despite all its great strength it cannot save. The horse is made ready for the day of battle, but victory rests with the Lord. Woe to those who go down to Egypt for help, who rely on horses, who trust in the multitude of their chariots and in the great strength of their horsemen, but do not look to the Holy One of Israel, or seek help from the Lord. I declare unto <u>name of person(s)</u>, let him/her/them who boasts boast about this: that he/she/they understand and know Me, that I am the Lord, who exercises kindness, justice and righteousness on earth, for in these I delight, declares the Lord. "The sword against her horses and chariots and all the foreigners in her rank! They will become women. A sword against her treasures! They will be plundered." Some boast of their chariots and horses, but I (we) boast in the name of the Lord, my (our) God. In Jesus' name, amen (Hebrews 4:16; Psalm 50:15; Luke 18:27; Psalms 136:12; Psalms 89:13; Psalms 118:15; Psalms 91:1-2; Isaiah 37:10; Psalms 62:11, Isaiah 43:13; Deuteronomy 17:16; Deuteronomy 20:1,4; 1 Chronicles 5:20; Psalms 22:4, 2; Chronicles 32:8; Psalms 33:17; Proverbs 21:31; Isaiah 31:1; Jeremiah 9:24; Jeremiah 50:37; Psalms 20:7).

CHAPTER FIFTEEN

DECEPTION OF TRUSTING IN MAN

Have you ever known someone who had a solid walk with the Lord and then at some point he or she decided to stop walking in godliness, stop listening to God's counsel, and started looking for help and counsel from somewhere else? Do you know this is the direct result of impatience with God's timing? Abraham and Sarah are great examples of being impatient with God's timing and taking matters into their own hands in order to help God along or bring the fulfillment of God's promise sooner (Genesis 15:2–6). They were promised a child, but Sarah became so impatient with the longing of a child that she gave her handmaiden Hagar to Abraham in order to produce an heir, Ishmael (Genesis 16). Ishmael, was not the son that God promised to them, Isaac was (Genesis 17:15–21). As a result, Hagar and Ishmael were sent away because Sarah feared that Ishmael would abuse Isaac, the promised son (Genesis 21:8–16). This also happened to the children of Israel. They would have cycles where they would follow God wholeheartedly and would listen to His every command and seek His counsel for help against their adversaries (Joshua 23–24; Judges 1:1–26). They would fall into sin (Judges 1:27–2:5, 10–17; Jeremiah 17:1–2; Jeremiah 18:12) and seek help elsewhere (Isaiah 31). The end result was always disastrous and would result in God judging them (Jeremiah 15:12–14; 16:16–19; 17:3–4) and their returning to Him humbly for assistance. Their best efforts failed them greatly (Judges 4:1–4), and their allies would always fail them too (Isaiah 31; Jeremiah 17:5–6; Hosea 14:3).

You may want to know, "Why did this happen?" They were trusting in their own strength and that of men rather than God's strength and help (Hosea 10:13; Psalm 33:16–17). Do you know we as believers can also fall into the same trap? We, too, at times are often deceived into thinking that our efforts or that of others, be it the rich and famous, the renowned, the brilliant, or others, can help us out of our dilemmas faster or more efficiently than God. What is the end result of this choice of looking elsewhere? Humiliation, having to repent to God, and say, "I am sorry. I wished I would have just listened and did it Your way, God" (Psalms 60:11; 108:12). That's why the Holy Scripture says that it's vain to look to man, princes, and to the arrogant for help (Psalms 118:8–9; Psalms 40:4; Psalms 146:3–4; Isaiah 2:22). Why? Because we are never really helped, and eventually we are back at the drawing board, confessing to God that we were wrong, repenting, and then waiting on God to help us (Micah 7:7–10).

A PRAYER OF DELIVERANCE FROM TRUSTING IN THE DECEPTION OF MEN

Lord, You said in Your Word that it is better to trust in the Lord than to put confidence in man, and Lord, I (we) place my (our) trust in You. "Be strong and courageous. Do not be afraid or discouraged because of the king of Assyria and the vast army with him, for there is a greater power with us then with him." Blessed is the man (woman) who makes the Lord his/her trust, who does not look to the proud, to those who turn aside to false gods. Give me (us) aid against the enemy, for the help of man is worthless. I say unto (name of person(s), "Do not put your trust in princes, in mortal men who cannot save." Woe to those who go down to Egypt for help, who rely on horses, who trust in the multitude of their chariots and in the great strength of their horsemen, but do not look to the Holy One of Israel, or seek help from the Lord. But the Egyptians are men and not God; their horses are flesh and not spirit. When the Lord stretches out His hand, he who helps will stumble, he who was helped will fall; both will perish together. When you cry out for help, let your collection of idols save you! The wind will carry all of them off, a mere breath will blow them away. But the man (woman) who makes You his (her) refuge will inherit the land and possess My holy mountain. This is what the Lord says: "Cursed is the one who trust in man, who depends on flesh for his (her) strength and whose heart turns away from the Lord." No man (woman) can be established in wickedness. Only in righteousness are you established. Repent and turn from your sins and do your first works over. Lord, create within name of person(s) a new clean heart and renew a rightful spirit within him/her/them. O Sovereign Lord! You made the heavens and the earth by Your strong and powerful arm. Nothing is too hard for You! You have all wisdom and do great and mighty miracles. You see the conduct of all people, and You give them what they deserve. "I am the Lord, the God of all the peoples of the world. Is there anything too hard for Me?" My people have turned their backs on Me and have refused to return. Even though I diligently taught them, they would not receive instruction or obey. And I will give them one heart and one purpose: to worship Me forever for their own good and for the good of all of their descendants. And I will make an everlasting covenant with them: I will never stop doing good for them. I will put a desire in their hearts to worship Me, and they will never leave Me. Then I will sprinkle clean water on you, and you will be clean. Your filth will be washed away, and you will no longer worship idols. And I will give you a new heart, and I will put a new spirit in you. I will take out your stony, stubborn heart and give you a tender, responsive heart. And I will put My Spirit in you so that you will follow My decrees and be careful to obey My regulations. Then you will remember your past sins and despise yourselves for all the detestable things you did. But remember," says the Sovereign Lord, "I'm not doing this because you deserve it. O, my people Israel, you should be utterly ashamed of all you have done! When I cleanse you from your sins, I will bring you home ... and rebuild the ruins." The Lord God says: Now the other nations taunt you, saying, 'Your Nation is a land that devours her people!' But they will not say this anymore. Your birth rate will rise, and your infant mortality rate will drop off sharply, says the Lord. No longer will those heathen nations sneer, for you will no longer be a nation of sinners, the Lord God says." In Jesus' name, amen (Psalms 118:8, 2 Chronicles 32:7; Psalms 40:4, Psalms 108:12, Psalms 146:3, Isaiah 31:1,3; 57:13; Jeremiah 17:5, Psalms 7:9, Psalms 75:10, Proverbs 2:21–22; Revelation 2:5; Psalms 51:10, Jeremiah 32:17, 19, Jeremiah 32:33, Jeremiah 32: 39-40, Ezekiel 36:25–27, Ezekiel 36:31–33, Ezekiel 36:13-15).

CHAPTER SIXTEEN

CHRISTIAN LIVING

Christian living is a life of freedom and not one full of rules and regulations (Galatians 5:1–6, 13). With that being said, it's not a life without constraints. There are guidelines that God has set in place to bring order and structure (Ephesians 5). The Christian life is one of balance and order (Ecclesiastes 7:15–18). We are modeling our lives after Christ, who led a balanced life of purpose while in His physical manifestation. He lived a life of love (John 11:32–36; John 13:1; Luke 7:11–17; 13:31–35; John 19:17-37), a life of forgiveness (Luke 5:17–24; 7:36–50; 23:33–43), a life full of goodness (Matthew 9:35), a life dedicated to helping others (John 4:1–42; 5:1–15; 8:1–11; Mark 5:1–20; Luke 9:10–17), a life as an intercessor(John 17:1–26; Luke 10:21–24), a life as a teacher (John 5:10–24; Mark 4; 7:1–23; Luke 11:1–13), a life as a carpenter (Mark 6:2–3), a life as a healer (John 4:43–54; 5:1–15; 9:1–34; Mark 3:1–6; 7:31–37), and a life of obedience (Luke 4:1–13; John 5:19,30; 6:38; 12:49–50; Matthew 26:39). He spent time with family and friends and had a very intimate relationship with the Father (John 2:1–12; Luke 2:41–50; Matthew 14:23; Luke 9:28-29; Matthew 3:13-17; Matthew 17:1–5). Although we are not perfect because all have sinned and fallen short of the glory of God (Romans 3:23), we must strive for perfection. We must have a perfect heart toward God (Matthew 5:48; Ephesians 5:1; Colossians 1:28; James 1:4). A good example of this is found in King David, who had a perfect heart toward God because he had a deep desire to please God (Psalms 19:14; 141:4; 119:8–11, 36–38). He always gave God thanks in all things (Psalms 118:27–29; Psalms 34:1-3). He was quick to repent whenever he was overtaken by a fault or sin, and he tried to live an upright life before God (Psalms 51, Psalms 32:1–6, 10–11; 25). This is how we are to live.

God wants us to live in such a way that it brings praise and reverence to His name (1 Peter 2:12; Matthew 9:8; John 15:8). We are exhorted in the Word of God to let our lights so shine before men that they will see our good works and glorify our Father in Heaven (Matthew 5:16). Our good works are our outward expression of our love and gratitude to God for all He did for us when He saved us and adopted us into the family of God (Titus 3:5; Galatians 6:10; Philippians 4:4–5; Galatians 5:13; 1 Timothy 2:2; Ephesians 1:5, 11). God desires that we be wise and live a steady life of goodness so that goodness will pour forth from our lives (Matthew 10:16; Romans 16:19; Colossians 4:5; James 3:13; Philippians 1:11). In addition, God desires for us to live good and pure lives (1 Thessalonians 4:3–8; 2 Thessalonians 2:13). Our lives should reflect a life of moderation, a love of truth and godly principles, agape, joy, peace, faith, holiness and righteousness, continual spiritual growth, and continual encouragement in the things of God, and should exhibit a Spirit-led life (Ecclesiastes 7:15–17; Philippians 1:9–10; Philippians 4:4; Mark 11:22; Colossians 3:1–3,11; Ephesians 4:23; Ephesians 5:17, 20; Colossians 3: 10; Philippians 4:10,15-17; Galatians 5:25). Our boast should be that of Christ and all He has done for us (Philippians 3:3). And as we mature in the faith we should be operating in the fruit of the Spirit and those who need further growth should be starting to develop the fruit of Spirit in their personal walk (Galatians 5:22–23).

PRAYER FOR CHRISTIAN LIVING

Dear Heavenly Father, I (we) pray that You will help Your people to continue in holiness and in founded biblical doctrine and to love one another as You have loved us. I (we) ask that You turn our hearts back to You and may we repent from turning away from You, our precious Savior. My (our) guilt has overwhelmed me (us) like a burden too heavy to bear. My (our) soul(s) are weary with sorrow; strengthen us according to Your Word. Keep us from deceitful ways; be gracious unto us through Your Law. Observed my commands and decrees that I delivered to you through My servants, the prophets. Fix your thoughts on what is true and good and right. Think about things that are pure and lovely, and dwell on the fine, good things in others. Think about all you can praise God for and be glad about that. Now your attitudes and thoughts must all be constantly changing for the better. Yes, you must be a new and different people, holy and good. Clothe yourself with this new nature. Do not cause the Holy Spirit sorrow by the way you live. Remember, He is the one who marks you to be present on that day when salvation from sin will be complete. For though once your heart was full of darkness, now it is full of light from the Lord, and your behavior should show it! Because of this light within you, you should do only what is good and right and true. Run from anything that gives you the evil thoughts that young people often have but stay close to anything that makes you want to do right. Have faith and love, and enjoy the companionship of those who love the Lord and have pure hearts. Lord, I (we) ask that You would bring influential older Christian men and women to mentor the younger men and younger women and urged them to behave carefully and take life seriously, and will be an example to these young men and young women of good deeds of every kind. Let everything we do reflect Your love of truth and the fact that we are dead earnest about it. May I (we) follow God's example in everything I (we) do just as much as a loved child imitates his/her father. May I (we) be full of love for others following the example of Christ, who loved us and gave Himself to God as a sacrifice to take away our sins. And God was pleased, for Christ's love for us was like sweet perfume to Him. Let there be no sex sin, impurity, or greed among any of us. Let no one be able to accuse us of such things as: dirty stories, foul talk, and coarse jokes— these are not for any of us. Instead, let us remind each other of God's goodness and be thankful. May we learn as we go along what pleases the Lord. May we not act thoughtlessly, but try to find out and do whatever the Lord wants us to do. May we not drink too much wine, for many evils lie along that path; may we be filled instead with the Holy Spirit, and controlled by Him. May we talk with each other much about the Lord, quoting Psalms and hymns and singing sacred songs, making music in our hearts to the Lord. May we always give thanks for everything to our God and Father in the name of our Lord Jesus Christ. Oh Lord God! You have made the heavens and the earth by Your great power; nothing is too hard for You. You have all wisdom and You do great and mighty miracles; for Your eyes are open to all the ways of men and You reward everyone according to his or her life deeds. "I am the Lord, the God of all mankind; is there anything too hard for Me?" Lord, give us one heart and mind to worship You forever for our own good and for the good of all our descendants. Lord, You promised to put a desire into our hearts to worship You so that we will never leave You. Then it will be as though You had sprinkled clean water on us, for we will be clean— our filthiness will be washed away, our idol worship gone. Lord, You, said that You would give us a new heart – and that You would give us a new and –right desires and put a new spirit within us. You said that You would take out our stony hearts of sin and give us new hearts of love. You, also, said that You would put Your Spirit within us so that we will obey Your laws and do whatever You command. Thank You, Abba Father, for being at work within us, helping us to want to obey You, and helping us to do what You want. In Jesus' name, amen (Luke 1:75; Acts 17:11; John 8:31; 5:12; Joel 2:12–13; Psalms 38:4; Psalms 119:28–29; 2Kings 17:13; Philippians 4:8; Ephesians 4:23–24, 30; 5:8; 2 Timothy 2:22; Titus 2:6–7; Ephesians 5:1-4,10,17-20, Jeremiah 32:17, 19, 27; 33:39–40; Ezekiel 36:25–27, 31–32, Philippians 2:13).

CHAPTER SEVENTEEN

REVELATION

God is a God who reveals secrets (Jeremiah 33:3; 2 Kings 6:8–12; Daniel 2:22, 47). Things that are hidden He will reveal if we ask (Luke 8:17; Matthew 10:26; Mark 4:22; Matthew 7:7). In the book of Daniel in chapter 2, King Nebuchadnezzar had a very puzzling dream that greatly disturbed him, and he consulted all of the wise men, magicians, and soothsayers in the entire Kingdom of Babylon and no one could tell him what he had dreamt or the dream's meaning. And because no one could tell King Nebuchadnezzar what he had dreamt or what the dream meant, he threatened to kill all the wise men in his kingdom. Daniel went home and sought God with his three friends Hananiah, Mishael, and Azariah for understanding and revelation of what King Nebuchadnezzar dreamt and the dream's meaning. And God revealed the dream to Daniel along with its interpretation. Likewise, we can ask God to give us understanding and revelation on very perplexing circumstances. We are exhorted in the Word of God to call upon Him, and He will show us great and mighty things which we do not know (Jeremiah 33:3). God is a revealer of dreams, of hidden counsel, and He will also reveal things to come. Elisha was a prophet used by God to reveal unto the Army of Israel the very secrets and plots of the King of Syria, even in his own private bed chambers (2 Kings 6:8–12). We are told that God will make us wiser than our enemies because He knows their thoughts from afar and will reveal them to us ahead of time (Psalms 119:98;2 Kings 6:8–12, Psalms 89:22).

Ezekiel was taken into the Spirit by God and was shown the corruption of the seventy elders of Israel in the inner courts of the Temple. God revealed to him their gross wickedness of idolatry and how they were leading the people of Israel into idolatry (Ezekiel 8). He also, showed Ezekiel the twenty-five prominent leaders who were responsible for giving all the wicked counsel to its citizens (Ezekiel 11:1–12). And God will do the same thing for us if we ask. Lastly, John the revelator was exiled on the island of Patmos and was taken up into the Spirit and he was shown what was to come– distant future. It was through this experience that we have the book of Revelation (Revelation 1:9; Revelation 1:1-2). God will show us things to come if we ask. Shall we ask?

PRAYER FOR REVELATION

O Heavenly Father, You are the revealer of hearts and secrets. We boldly approach Your Throne of Grace, asking that my (our) <u>loved one(s) name(s)</u> be given the revelatory knowledge and understanding right now that a man's and woman's ways are in full view of the Lord and that He examines all his/her/their paths. Nothing in all creation is hidden from God's sight. Everything is uncovered and laid bare before the eyes of Him to whom we must give an account. I ask, Lord, that You expose and bring to light any action, thought, sin, deception, wrong affiliation, wrong association, conflict, behavior, deeds that is contrary to your plan, purposes, and will for <u>loved one(s)'</u> life (lives) and bring it to his/her/their awareness right now so it can be repented of, confessed, and forsaken. Give him/her/them the understanding that there is nothing hidden that will not be revealed and nothing in darkness that will not be brought to the light. And when they attempt to hide things that are necessary for us and others who are in God-ordain relationships with them, let them be given the understanding it will be exposed. In Jesus' name, amen (Daniel 2:22; Hebrews 4:16; 11:1; Proverbs 5:21; Hebrews 4:13; Jeremiah 16:17; 23:24; Daniel 2:22; Psalm 19:12; Luke 8:17; Mark 4:22).

CHAPTER EIGHTEEN

FORGIVENESS

We are admonished in the Word of God to forgive as Christ for gave us (Ephesians 4:32). Jesus shared a parable in Matthew 18 about a king who had a debtor who owed him an outstanding debt in the excess of $10,000,000. But the debtor had no way of paying his debt, so the king ordered that he along with his wife and children be sold in order to compensate for his debt. The man then began to plead with the king and begged for forgiveness. Then the man assured the king he would in fact pay off his debt. It was at this point that the king felt pity for him and decided to cancel his debt and release him from the debtor prison. Shortly, after he was released, he ran into a man who owed him $2,000 and demanded that the man immediately repay the $2,000. The man begged and pleaded with him, the man whom the king had recently forgiven, to be patient with him so that he could have the time to repay him. But the released man objected and ordered the man to repay him the $2,000 on the spot. When the king found out about what the man whom he had forgiven had done, the king became angry and threw the debtor back in prison until he paid off the total amount of his original debt. This is an allegory about what will happen to us if we do not forgive. Our outstanding debt of sin was paid in full on Calvary. It was a debt that none of us could afford to pay, and Jesus, the King of kings, graciously paid it for both you and I. He did it out of mercy and love. Forgiveness is a personal choice that will greatly impact our lives.

Whether we choose to forgive or hold unto unforgiveness, there are consequences for both. There is a direct correlation between the kind of quality of life that you will experience if you choose to forgive or choose not to forgive. Those who choose to forgive often have much fuller and rewarding lives than those who live by unforgiveness. Also, those who choose to forgive are usually more joyful, thankful and grateful, and they experience a greater sense of peace than those who choose to do otherwise. Conversely, our spiritual lives are significantly impacted by our ability or inability to forgive. When we choose to forgive, it enables God's blessings to flow readily in our lives, but when we refuse to forgive, it inhibits God's blessings from flowing into our lives (Mark 11:25). In addition, forgiveness or the lack of thereof will either enable or prohibit us from receiving forgiveness from God (Matthew 6:14). Lastly, forgiveness is not condoning the actions of other's against us. Oh, quite the contrary. It's a freeing act that keeps us from developing a root of bitterness and hatred, thus keeping us in love and unity with one another (Romans 12:19–20; Colossians 3:13–14; Hebrews 12:14–15). Forgiveness is a conduit that releases God to intervene in our lives (Leviticus 19:18; Deuteronomy 32:35; Proverbs 24:29; 1 Samuel 26:10–11). Shall we pray?

PRAYER FOR FORGIVENESS

Dear Heavenly Father, I (we) ask that name(s) learn to forgive as Christ forgave him/her/them and that he/she/they be given right now the revelatory knowledge and understanding that when holding grudges and refusing to forgive others hinders God's blessings from flowing into his/her/their life (lives). You said, if you forgive men their trespasses, Your Heavenly Father will also forgive you (us). But if you do not forgive men their trespasses, neither will Your Heavenly Father forgive you of your trespasses and if your brother (sister) sins against you seven times in a day and comes to you seven times and says, "I repent," you are to forgive him (her). I (we) pray that You, Lord, would enable name(s) to let all bitterness, wrath, anger, clamor, and evil speaking be put away from you, with all malice. And be kind to one another, just as God in Christ also forgave you. And may name(s) know that blessed are the merciful, for they shall obtain mercy, and may name(s) learn to show mercy so that he/she/they may obtain mercy. You said, that You, Lord, show mercy to the merciful and You show Yourself merciless to the merciless. In Jesus' name, amen (Ephesians 5:10; Philippians 1:9–11; Ephesians 4:32; Daniel 2: 22; Matthew 6:15; Luke 17:4; Ephesians 4:31-32; Matthew 5:7; Psalms 18:25; James 2:13).